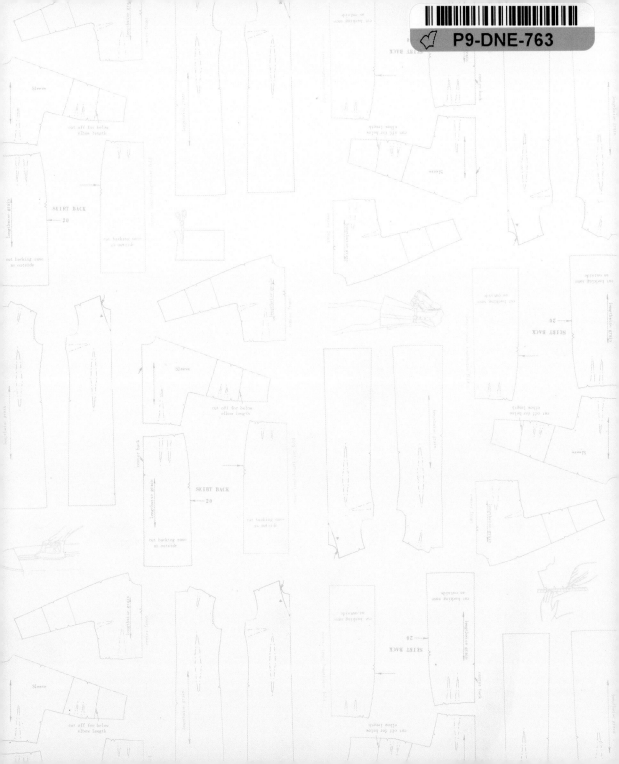

My Mom
STYLE ICON

Piper Weiss

My Mom
STYLE ICON
Piper Weiss

CHRONICLE BOOKS
SAN FRANCISCO

※◇◇◇◇◇◇◇◇◇◇◇◇◇◇◇◇◇◇◇◇◇◇◇◇◇◇◇◇◇◇◇※

For my mom, and all the mothers in this book,
who put up with us as teenagers.

And for my dad, who knew a style icon
the minute he saw one.

※◇◇◇◇◇◇◇◇◇◇◇◇◇◇◇◇◇◇◇◇◇◇◇◇◇◇◇◇◇◇◇※

Library of Congress Cataloging-in-Publication Data is available.

ISBN: 978-0-8118-7881-4

Manufactured in China

Design by Jake Gardner and Sarah Pulver

Photos are courtesy of the subjects or contributors listed
unless otherwise indicated throughout.

10 9 8 7 6 5 4 3 2 1

Chronicle Books LLC
680 Second Street
San Francisco, CA 94107
www.chroniclebooks.com

Table of Contents

Introduction 6

1 Let's Bring Back:
Treasures from the Attic 11

2 Hair Story:
A Brief History of Big Hairdos 33

3 Moms Gone Wild:
Rebels, Ragers, and Road Warriors 51

4 The Originals:
From the People Who Brought
You Everything You Wear Now 69

5 Going to the Chapel:
The Only Dress That Ever Mattered 90

6 Lucky Dads:
Fashion for Better or for Worse 107

7 Mommy and Me:
Growing Up with an Icon 123

8 Moms Away!:
Sisterhood of the Traveling Pantsuits 137

Acknowledgments 156

Introduction

ENTER ANY DEPARTMENT STORE CHANGING ROOM, AND you're bound to hear the same two phrases: "Try it on" and "I don't want to, Mom." As humans, we're hard-wired to rebel against our parents and control our children. And this species malfunction is most obvious during shopping trips. At least that was my experience. I never wanted to dress like my mom. She didn't know me or where I was coming from and so on and so forth.

And then one day, everything changed. I mean everything.

I had a wedding to attend, and I needed a fancy purse—the kind without strings or straps that you have to hold in your palm all night—the kind that can only fit a few nickels, and—if you're lucky—a tampon. The kind only moms own. Rifling through my mother Marilyn's closet, a collector of these props, I accidentally pulled out a

crocheted belt from the '60s. I dug a little deeper and came across a suede fringe vest. Both were items I'd been coveting in stores—the knockoff versions, of course. And here I was in the presence of the real thing. I asked my mom when they were from. Her replies: "Oh, that's from a SoHo boutique. I used to wear that when I was an art student at NYU."

"That? I wore that to a party in the West Village in the late '60s. I remember Barry Gibb was holding court by an indoor swimming pool in the middle of the living room. Lots of pot smoke."

Wait . . . what?

My digs through the years eventually led me to the mother lode: two white photo albums stuffed with pictures that I found tucked in a cabinet in my parents' living room. When I slipped the first one from its hiding place, a brittle, faded snapshot fell out. Mom?

"Oh, that's when I went to Jamaica for the weekend with my friend."

"For the weekend?"

"My rent was low; things were reasonable back then. If there was a great last-minute deal, my friend and I would just take off. We stayed at the Playboy Club in Ocho Rios. It was a total party scene."

"Is that an arm cuff you're wearing . . . and a cigarette in your hand?"

"Oh, yes. And I remember I just picked up that hat from a little store in the town there."

"Who is that soldier ogling you?"

"There were always guys just hanging around."

Who is this woman, and what did she do with my mother? I wondered. And more to the point, can I borrow those bell-bottoms?

With each picture I examined, I found more treasures: caftans, chained belts, hair pieces, fake round-framed glasses, false eyelashes, embroidered blazers, mod mini-dresses. Camels, even.

"When were you in Morocco, Mom?"

"Oh, I don't know—'67? '68?"

It's not that I didn't know my mother had a past; I just didn't realize there was so much of it. And that it was so good looking. I'd been trying for years to acquire the femme fatale hairstyle she flaunted in the pictures. I collected bracelets for months to pull off the kind of arm accessory she let dangle in front of the camera effortlessly. And the men? I didn't even know they made them like that.

I realized then that I will turn into my mother. If I'm lucky.

Let me reassure you that Mom and I weren't always on the same page when it came to style. Here is a brief history of our relationship:

Age 5: I cut off all my hair to play Hansel in an impromptu staging of Hansel and Gretel in my bedroom. Mom flips out, taking complete and permanent control of my follicles. Teaches me her age-old technique of hot rollers and bobby pins.

Age 7: Mom—an "Annie Hall" doppelganger—dresses me like she dresses herself—red and blue turtlenecks, oxford shirts with popped collars. I'd rather wear pink tutus.

Age 13: Mom and I battle over my bat mitzvah dress but come to one agreement—pinning gym socks into the bosom so it fits.

Age 15: We engage in a period of mutual hatred stemming from polar visions of what kinds of clothing I look good in.

Age 18: Mom's silk scarf collection now requires two drawers. Meanwhile, as a freshman in college, I cultivate a single dreadlock and pierce my eyebrow. Big mistake.

Age 19: Thrift stores have become my way of life. Meanwhile, as Mom's modern wardrobe grows, her collection of vintage fashions are lodged in an unreachable closet shelf, unbeknownst to me.

Age 25: I discover her vintage scarves, belts, and jewelry. Her stuff is more authentic and in better shape than anything in a store.

Age 30: I find her old pictures and covet everything in them. Dressed in the pieces I've adopted over the years, looking like a more attractive version of me, our relationship boils down to a fashion page in *US Weekly*: She wore it better.

Those pictures triggered a life-altering revelation—the kind that compels a daughter to start, and more importantly maintain, a blog. I'd spent the past few years editing fashion and lifestyle articles for the *New York Daily News*, where I'd insert the term "style icon" in stories about Audrey Hepburn, Grace Kelly, Angelina Jolie. Finally, I'd found my own. The blog My Mom, the Style Icon

began as a tribute to Marilyn's buried fashion past. But everyone I showed it to would insist that his or her mom had some incredible style, too. They weren't exaggerating.

Submissions piled up from around the world, including Canada, Iran, Ireland, and Chile. While the countries, eras, and fashions varied, the subtext of the submissions was the same: awe. It was as if people were emerging from an apocalyptic cloud of smoke, each holding a picture of her mom, saying "It all makes sense now."

One of the first e-mails I received was from a daughter whose mother grew up in Croatia in the '60s. In addition to describing the schoolgirl wool skirt and sweater getup she wore, the writer added: "My mother had a turbulent relationship with her mom, so she moved to Canada when she was just twenty years old to make a new start for herself." Another submission showed a mom flaunting her long legs in high-waisted shorts in 1968. The story goes: "She sent this to my dad when he was stationed in Vietnam right after they were married. It kept getting stolen from his stuff, so she had to keep reprinting it and sending it again." One mom was a dancer on *The Dean Martin Variety Show*. Another ran away from her strict Texas family to get hitched.

Photo submissions became homages, memorial tributes, boasts, and, in some cases, apologies to mothers. It's hard to imagine your mom as a person, even less a teenager, unless you see photo evidence. It's like meeting a different person—one you may have been friends with. All of the pictures in the following pages were submitted by people who made that monumental discovery and learned a valuable lesson in the process. Style isn't just about the clothes; it's about the way they are worn. That's to say, with no regrets.

1

Let's Bring Back:
Treasures from the Attic

True story: I once simultaneously wore the following items: a scarf fastened with a cameo broach, a floppy 1970s wide-brimmed felt hat, and a pair of round oversized sunglasses. Oh, and I had a magnifying glass dangling from a gold chain around my neck. Here is what someone told me: "You know that famous saying, 'Before you leave the house, remove one accessory'? Well, you need to remove three." He was right. But I was only trying to give accessories the kind of showcase our mothers and grandmothers were famous for. So how come they could do it without public ridicule? That's a question with a chicken/egg–type answer. Are we less tolerant of hats, pins, and scarves because we don't wear them as well as our moms? Or do we not wear them as well as our moms simply because we are less tolerant?

I think my own major misstep was a lack of confidence. I was doing a lot of tacit, "Huh? Huh? What do you think?" facial expressions—something any mom would frown upon. If you're going to wear something, say our mothers, you'd better own it. They weren't just talking about our teen kleptomania stage. They were talking about not apologizing for bold fashion statements. And throughout the decades, there have been many: cloches, trilbys, brooches, muffs. These are English words, we just haven't used them much lately. It's time they made a comeback.

HATS 101

The '90s had trucker hats. The '00s had modernized fedoras. The '40s, '50s, '60s, and '70s had everything else: straw, felt, wool, floppy, firm, feathered, veiled. Back then, the rule was written in stone: Wear the hat; don't let it wear you. These days, baseball caps and modified fedoras are code for a bad hair day or a herpes outbreak. For our foremothers, a hat served a very different purpose: It was a dramatic frame for the face and a cake topper to a meticulously conceived outfit. But before you bust open the door to your local haberdasher, consider a few lessons from the originators.

The Wide-Brimmed Straw Bonnet

Mom: Irene Coon Royder
Granddaughter: Jennifer Maddox Plesko
Era: 1925, Texas

"My grandmother, at left, pictured with her sister, was a bit of a rebel, at least for deep south Texas," says granddaughter Jennifer. "After this picture was taken in the 1930s, she cut off her hair and moved off the farm and into a boarding house in the booming metropolis of Bryan, where she got a job working for the United States Department of Agriculture. She didn't get married and have my mom until she was forty."

The Wide-Brimmed Fedora

Mom: Kathy Ramirez
Son: Erick Cifuentes
Era: Early 1970s, Bogotá, Colombia

The Tulle Topper

Mom: Marie Castleberry
Daughter: Sandy Lynn Davis
Era: Late 1950s, Chicago

"They don't make bridesmaid ensembles like
they used to! In this photo, my mom is on
the way to a friend's wedding, and I just
love all of the picture-perfect accessories:
gloves, clutch, and especially that hat!
(The car isn't bad either.) But of course,
it's her terrific poise that pulls everything
together and makes it all look somehow
effortless."

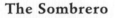

The Sombrero

Mom: Homa Nassirizadeh
Daughter: Roya Nassirizadeh
Era: 1972, Maryland

Homa knew how to turn heads into head-
turners. Sometimes she employed an oversized
sombrero. Other times she used her hands.
"My mother moved to the States from Iran with
little knowledge of the culture and barely
any English," says Roya. "She went to beauty
school and got a job at one of the leading
hair salons in the Washington, D.C., area."
Her artistry with hair, heavily influenced
by her native country, was a hit with the
politicos. "She would get picked up from her
salon and transported to the White House to
do Lady Bird Johnson's hair. Not a lot has
changed as she continues to style the hair
of political figures like Colin and Alma
Powell and Andy and Kathy Card."

The Trilby

Mom: Georgia Bloch
Daughter: Julie Bloch
Era: Late 1940s, Europe

"This photo was taken in Paris on a trip with my father, who was the son
of one of the owners of the department store where my mom worked," says
Julie. In 1949, thirty-two-year-old Georgia wasn't just following women's
fashion, she was dictating it. As an illustrator of stylebooks and an
artist for a Philadelphia department store, Bloch drew what women wanted
to look like. And she dressed that way, too.

The Formal Straw Hat

Mom: Roisin Durkin
Daughter: Ellen Durkin
Era: 1950s, Ireland

"It would have been unusual for women and men in those days to leave the house without a hat," says Ellen. "For a formal function like a wedding, Mom would always have a new hat and, as a result, she grew an impressive collection over fifty years."

The Cloche

Mom: Mary Carter
Daughter: Lucy Carter
Era: Early 1970s, Surrey, England

JUMPSUITS AND HOTPANTS

Dresses are lifesavers: They eliminate the mixing and matching that can make it impossible to get out of the house. But wouldn't they be even better if they came with pants? Presumably this was how the inventor of jumpsuits first stumbled on a gold mine. It takes a brave woman to pull it off well. Jumpsuits highlight your haunches and don't always break properly at your waistline. They also are reminiscent of a circus performer. But dang it if they aren't the most comfortable game in town. On the other end of the spectrum are hot pants: half the material, a fraction of the comfort level—but just as rewarding in their own little way.

Mom: Mindy Lewis
Son: Michael Lewis
Era: 1970, Pittsburgh, Pennsylvania

Mindy wore this jumpsuit the day her husband returned from his tour in Vietnam, which was when this photo was taken. She had had her second child, Michael, when he was overseas, and she wanted to show off her svelte figure upon his arrival. The twenty-five-year-old mom purchased the suit at the local mall and came home to make mini pizzas from canned biscuits for the welcome-home party. Michael, who was six months old when he met his dad for the first time, observes the jumpsuit's effect on his mother: "Looking at this picture now, I realize I've never seen her stand that way. She looks so confident. She must have been feeling good about the way she looked."

Mom: Elizabeth Filardo
Daughters: Lauren & Lisa Acinapura
Era: Early 1970s, New Jersey

Elizabeth is known as Aunt Booty
to her nieces and nephews. This
white suit, with short-shorts buried
underneath, may be used to trace the
origin of the nickname.

Mom: Eva Peglow
Daughter: Katja Peglow
Era: 1970s, Warsaw, Poland

"My dad took this picture during their
honeymoon," says Katja. "She was twenty-
three then, and picked this particular
outfit because it was comfortable and
khaki was all the rage."

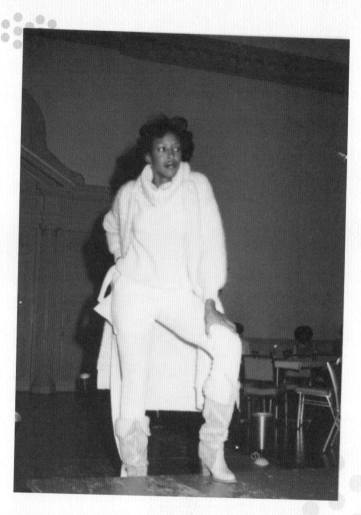

Mom: Connie Fogg-Jenkins
Daughter: Jasmine Jenkins
Era: Late 1970s, Illinois

Not technically a jumpsuit, but it's impossible to tell where one item of clothing ends and
another begins—booties and all. "The photo was taken October 28, 1978 at a fashion show for my
mom's sorority Delta Sigma Theta," says Jasmine, whose mom was in her junior year at University
of Illinois Urbana-Champaign at the time of the event. "The fashion show was a fundraiser, and
local vendors agreed to donate clothing. My mother put the outfit together herself. It's amazing
it came together so well from the limited shopping choices available in the area at the time.
I think the attitude captured in the pose really helps make the outfit."

THE PARTY TOPPERS

When decorative pins are replaced by Bluetooth headsets and cell-phone belt clips, you know we have a problem. Technology may have advanced, but our flair for unique accessories certainly hasn't. For a formal night out, consider a simple bow or a not-so-simple flower arrangement.

photo courtesy of the Whittingham family

The Clutch

Mom: Jean Whittingham
Daughter: Beth Goehring
Era: 1958, Chicago

The Brooch

Mom: Suzanne Kovacs
Daughter: Anne-Marie Kovacs
Era: 1967, Canada

The Dangly Earrings

Mom: Leonora Ivnitskaya
Daughter: Alla Ivnitskaya
Era: 1960s, Former USSR

The Corsage

Mom: Ruth Royder Maddox
Daughter: Jennifer Maddox Plesko
Era: 1968, Texas

Portola Studio–S.F.

The Headband

Mom: Natasza Dimmock
Daughter: Jessica Dimmock
Era: Early 1960s, New York

WHEN TURTLENECKS WERE KING

Turtlenecks hide hickeys, elongate your silhouette, and eliminate the need for a wool scarf. They're chicken soup for the mom's neck. And they ruled the world of fashion in the '60s and '70s. Audrey Hepburn turned women on to black, tight turtlenecks, and soon the item was being tucked into skirts and bell-bottoms and applied to sweater dresses and wedding gowns. The law of ladies' blouses states: the more cleavage, the sexier. But the high-necked shirt or dress is the one exception. If worn correctly—tightly and with ballerina posture—it may cause complete man-magnetism.

Mom: May-Lis Gronlund
Daughter: Melissa Gronlund
Era: 1970s, Zermatt, Switzerland

"I have no idea why my mom is only half dressed,"
says Melissa. But she got the important half right.

Mom: Betsy Nason
Daughter: Margot Nason
Era: 1972, Salisbury, Maryland

In the 1970's, Betsy (with her husband, John) had an endless supply of colorful turtlenecks. "She wore them a lot with hip-hugger jeans, which she also had a lot of, apparently," says Margot. It was not your classic suburban fare, so Betsy would trek to Georgetown, to the one boutique that carried the cut she craved.

Mom: May Wong
Daughter: Lisa Wong Jackson
Era: Late 1960s

"This is one of my favorite photos of my mom when she was a teenager.
The white turtleneck belted dress is so stylish and goes perfectly
with the pose and record player."

GOLDEN GLOVES ERA

It's impossible to pinpoint the exact date that "indoor" gloves fell out of fashion. It was a gradual exit. Stevie Nicks took the tips off her gloves. Madonna lost the hands altogether in favor of arm warmers. Then Michael Jackson just took one entire glove off. We should have known then that the other was bound to follow. In the '40s, and '50s, and even '60s, gloves were just like bracelets. Only fancier. If you had a wedding, a prom, or just a Friday night date, you had better bring your second hands.

Mom: Judy Posch
Daughter: Brooke Posch
Era: Early 1960s, Long Island, New York

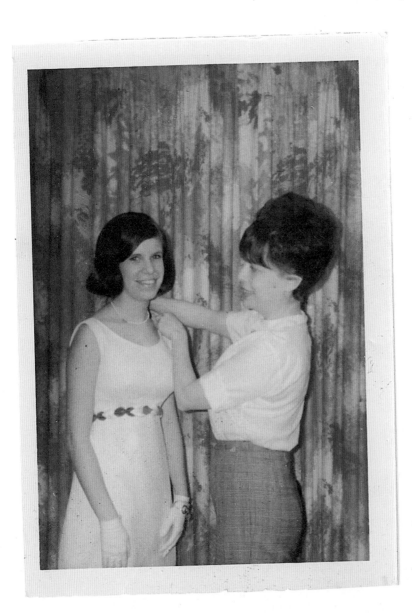

Mom: Roberta Steinberg
Daughter: Doree Shafrir
Era: 1966, Massachusetts

CIRCLES OF LIFE

Of all the shapes that glasses have taken—square, rectangular, cat-eyed—round may be the most underrated. Circular rims have become synonymous with John Lennon, Tommy Chong, and last-minute hippie Halloween costumes. But in reality, they were far more popular than that. Well into the '70s, women—and The Ramones—were rewriting the rules of round-rimmed glasses.

Mom: Audrey Both
Daughter: Amanda Both
Era: Early 1970s

photo by Larry Wolfinsohn, courtesy of the Wolfinsohn family

Mom: Susan Wolfinsohn
Son: Ben Wolfinsohn
Era: 1970s, the Midwest

Mom: Suellen Cox
Daughter: Hannah Debree
Era: Late 1960s

"I love everything about this photo of my mom; it evokes summertime and easy happiness. I love her big smile and side ponytails, that she's riding a cool bike while sporting such a stylish outfit, and those big Jackie-O glasses!"

my mom,
THE COLLECTOR

WHEN THEY WENT TO THE ROMANCE CONVENTIONS, SUSIE Felber's mother always commanded the biggest lines. As the author of over thirty works of historical fiction, Edith Layton had an avid readership who flocked to the annual group book signings in auditoriums around the country. In person, the author didn't disappoint either. Unlike the other writers who attended these events to push copies of their books with busty, besotted women on the covers, Susie's mother actually looked like the characters she wrote about. Capes, bust-baring gowns, bejeweled clutches, and red lipstick were part of her presentation.

Last year, after Edith lost her battle with ovarian cancer, Susie found herself digging through a mountain of vintage purses in an attempt to sort through her mother's belongings. "She had at least thirty; who needs thirty evening bags?"

Someone who has a fan collection to match. Edith's boudoir boasted everything from the whale-boned to ostrich-feathered. In decor they matched her Victrola, Tiffany lamp, and Edison phone. "The interior of her house was chock-a-block with antiques," says Susie. That was a sharp contrast to the exterior—a standard single-family house on Long Island. "My mother never imagined she'd be a suburban housewife," says Susie. More surprising was that she maintained her eccentricities in spite of the '70s suburbia. Or because of it.

The daughter of Jewish immigrants, Edith was raised in Forest Hills, Queens, in the '40s. There was little money for clothes, so she had to safety pin her underwear when the elastic wore thin. But by the time she moved to New York, she'd developed her own eclectic style: part Audrey Hepburn, part '60s beatnik. She dated high-minded celebrities like Peter Falk and *Rosemary's Baby* author Ira Levin. "She almost married him, but he didn't

want her to write. He said 'Women can create such great things with their bodies, why would they want to waste it on writing?' That was when she said, 'Buh-bye.'"

Soon after this, Edith met Susie's dad, a young doctor who had just returned from Korea. "She thought he was an ailing veteran. She would never have initially married a Jewish doctor. It was too predictable for her." But falling in love made her do crazy things—like move to Long Island. There, she laid down roots and began publishing her romance novels.

Soon her heroines began to develop their own sartorial side. Obsessed with the Regency period in England in the 1800s, she traveled to London to research the clothing of that time. "My mother loved dressing her characters. The clothes were just as important going on as they were coming off." When she was able to direct the artists on the covers, she'd send pictures from the period detailing what she'd imagine the heroine to wear. It was something most romance authors didn't do.

Edith was just as decisive when it came to her own daughter's clothing. With two brothers, Susie was a harbor for her mother's vintage passions in real life.

"She used me as a dress up doll. I was a tomboy climbing trees in these incredible dresses with matching hats." The only period of dress Edith hated to see her daughter in was the '50s. "If I wore a '50s poodle skirt or sweater, she would turn her nose up. She thought the '50s were too restrained and bad for women—it was way too much about conformity." Edith's 1970s green suede suit on the other hand projected just the opposite.

In a vintage dress, right out of one of her novels in 1975.

In a green suede suit outside of her home on Long Island in 1978.

Dressed to match her antique lamp in 1966.

2

Hair Story:
A Brief History of Big Hairdos

If you ask any mom what her desert island outfit would be, she'll likely say a hairbrush. More than any little black dress, hair is the ultimate costume. It can make you taller, thinner, and more glamorous. It's also a good place to store a lifetime supply of bobby pins. Moms are no schlubs in the technology department either. My own mother—who can't turn on a computer without thinking she broke it—could occupy a scalp with an army of electromagnetic hot rollers in 5 minutes flat. The next generation can't even compete. Maybe that's why some of the highest hairstyles haven't held up.

HIGH AND MIGHTY

In the early '60s, First Lady Jackie Kennedy, the arbiter of all things fancy, challenged young women to raise their heads high. It's not what she intended, but pretty soon, bouffants, bumps, and beehives were towering atop many a lady's noggin. More than just trends, they were stratospheres. These days you have to hit up a senior prom to spot the handiwork. But back in the '60s, all you had to do was enter the girl's bathroom at a local high school to find hordes of women spraying, coiffing, and teasing their follicles with combs and barrels of Aqua Net.

Mom: Gloria Ferri
Daughter: Tara Ferri
Era: 1965, Schenectady, New York
Height: 4–6 inches

This was not one of those wake-up-and-go looks. You're looking at the woman who earned the title of "biggest hair" in her senior yearbook. "My mother has very fine hair, so to get this look, she spent hours with curlers, teasing the back of it and then smoothing over the top layer with curlers and hairspray," says Tara. "She would run to the bathroom during breaks from class and give her hair a spritz to keep the volume. My dad remembers it being a rat's nest underneath the top layer."

JUL

Mom: Di Oliver
Daughter: Hatty Oliver
Era: 1963, Gloucestershire, United Kingdom
Height: Off the charts

"I've always had very thick hair—all I did was set it in big rollers.
I never needed to tease or back comb it," says Di. "I was very tall,
so having a lot of hair balanced my shape."

Mom: Gail Horlick
Daughter: Rachel Horlick
Era: 1967, Queens, New York
Height: 5 inches

It was her prom, what do you expect?

Mom: Urai Staples
Daughter: Anna Rice
Era: 1966, Thailand
Height: 5–6 inches

How does a new mom have time to build the Tower of Babel on her
head? "She had her own personal stylist that came to her home
to massage, wash, and style her hair for her. All of her clothes
were tailor-made, too. I still have most of her wardrobe from
this time, and it's amazing," says Anna.

The Beehive

Mom: Janine Piniarski
Daughter: Dorothy Piniarski
Era: Early 1960s, England

The Beehive Supreme

Mom: Stella Ignatovsky
Daughter: Meital Ignatovsky
Era: 1960s, Israel

The Extreme Chignon

Mom: Meryl Rizzotti
Daughter: Alessandra Rizzotti
Era: Early 1970s

The Pompadour

Mom: Dora Evelyn Cobb
Great Granddaughter: Jennifer Lawson
Era: 1939, somewhere in America

At twenty-nine, Dora already had three sons—the first
at thirteen. She was constantly moving from town to
town during the Depression as her husband looked for
work, says Jennifer. Despite this fact, she still put
Bettie Page to shame.

scrapbook,
LINDA'S MEGA MANE

MELISSA SMITH MALLERY THINKS HER MOM IS AN ICON of epic hair proportions. "Go big or go home. That's always been a motto for us," she says. It was also a motto of the '80s, a decade that defined Linda Smith's teenage years in Kentucky. Now a criminal defense attorney, Linda still holds herself and her hair to the credo. Melissa takes us on a historical tour.

"She was then, and is still, a big fan of the hot roller. She'd always poof her hair up before she'd leave the house, and I'd think it was too big, but she'd insist it would fall."

"This was taken before a 'dress-up' day at her high school. She dressed up as one of the B52s."

"At sixteen she was a teen model, so this is one of her modeling shots. She was very critical of her bangs; she never thought they feathered correctly."

FLIP IT

Sometime in the '60s, a mandate came down from the higher-ups that hair should no longer curl in toward the neck, but out. And so it came to pass that millions of women had to endure the rigorous process known as 'The Flip,' which often meant sleeping overnight in large, prickly rollers.

Mom: Debbie Rumbaugh Lucas
Daughter: Erin Blair Gobin
Era: 1970s, Texas

Mom: Kathy Acquisto
Daughter: Selena Metts
Era: 1968, New Jersey

"The picture, her high-school yearbook photo, was taken in 1968, a year before she attended Woodstock," says Selena. At the time, she was gathering fashion inspiration from regular trips to the folk-rock mecca of the planet—Greenwich Village.

Mom: Joyce Venet Gross
Daughter: Jennifer Halon
Era: 1963

Mom: Peggy Schapiro
Son: Andrew Schapiro
Era: Mid 1960s

"A few years ago, I found this portrait of my mom from her senior year in high school and was struck by how little has changed about her natural beauty over the years. She still wears her thick blonde hair at shoulder length and exhibits a sense of grace and elegance down to the details."

The Flesh

Mom: Julie Wood
Daughter: Jennifer Lawson
Era: 1981, Lemon Grove, California

The Waterfall Wisps

Mom: Karen Ann Willert
Daughter: Kathy Willert
Era: 1981, San Diego, California

"Her hair was permed and colored with henna," says Kathy.
"She's naturally light brown like I am, although red was
such a fantastic color for her."

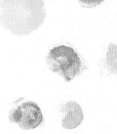

Rockabilly Bangs

Mom: Georgia Bloch
Daughter: Julie Bloch
Era: Early 1950s, Philadelphia, Pennsylvania

Georgia's artistic side showed in her perfectly manicured cut. "She illustrated a book in 1954 for the John Roberts Powers modeling schools called *Secrets of Charm*. It is filled with pen-and-ink drawings of all things pertaining to being a woman in the early 1950s," says Julie. "She later entered into a more 'bohemian' period where I remember her wearing a mink coat and tennis shoes, campaigning for John Kennedy. She was quite a woman."

SHORT 'N' SWEET

Cutting off all your hair is a defining moment. Practically, all that time spent blow-drying and obsessing can now be spent on more productive endeavors. An act such as this is usually paired with a new adventure, a career change, or a life decision. Spiritually, it's a reexamination of priorities. Long locks are a classic symbol of femininity. Whether it's true or false, the origin of this idea is that men love long hair. A super-short style is arguably akin to bra burning. The message sent is, "Who cares what men like?" Unfortunately that backfires, since men love that message.

The Pixie

Mom: Judie Silcox
Daughter: Andrea Silcox
Era: 1969, San Francisco

In 1967, Mia Farrow had world-famous hairstylist Vidal Sassoon chop off her locks for her signature waif cut. Two years later, Judie Silcox proved brunettes do it better. "It was definitely the haircut of the modern wash-and-wear woman," says Judie who, like Mia, had her pixie perfected at Vidal Sassoon's salon. "The picture was taken by my then-fiancé. I lived in San Francisco, and he was visiting and of course we were taking my favorite mode of transportation—the cable car."

The Perma-fro

Mom: Jane Gallagher
Daughter: Erica Burke
Era: Early 1980s, Illinois

Erica was two years old when her mother, Jane, stopped straightening her hair with a flat iron. "In 1980 she cut her hair and went back to her natural curls." After years of wearing wigs and burning her scalp for the coveted stick-straight locks, curls finally made a cultural comeback.

"Afros were trendy then, and I wanted something different," says Jane. "I got lots of compliments."

IN 1965, PERLEY MAE DAVIDSON GOT A HAIRCUT UNLIKE any other. Jagged, tufted, spiked, and cropped—a high-concept symphony of hairstyles unique to this earth. Or, at least, to the Chicago area.

"Of all the looks I've seen of hers over the years, this is my favorite," says daughter Heather Davidson.

There were a lot of looks. "I used to tell her she was the only person who had fifteen curling irons at any given time in her bathroom," says Heather. "She grew up in a large, poor family and had to wear hand-me-down clothes most of her early years. I guess she always had control of her hair, no matter the budget."

3

Moms Gone Wild:
Rebels, Ragers, and Road Warriors

When your mother tells you she was a free spirit back in the day, she means it. She may not have had a quickie Vegas wedding or have created a homemade bong out of a pineapple. But then again, she may have. You just have to ask. Pictures tell a thousand words—even if they don't tell the whole story. A snapshot of her in a barely-there bikini or posing next to her very first love—a Mustang—is a clue that her life wasn't always family dinners and PTA meetings. That devil-may-care attitude deserves to be toasted—with a whiskey. Champagne is for pussies.

THE MOTORHEADS

Women drivers. Those two words were fodder for every would-be comedian in the '50s. Not only were the jokes about a lady's lack of vehicular coordination not funny, they were false. But that didn't change the fact that getting behind the wheel left women subject to ridicule. Despite that fact, in collecting photos of mothers, the single biggest accessory in snapshots across the board was the car (or motorcycle). The mothers in this book would not stand to be backseat drivers.

Mom: Vidyawati Sooknanan
Daughter: Kiran Keeshan
Era: 1981, Long Island, New York

"We drove my sister's Pontiac Firebird from Montreal to Long Island—an eight-hour trip. We were going to visit our brother, and it was my first time in America," remembers Vidyawati, a native of Trinidad, who was seventeen at the time. "When we arrived, my sister pulled out a camera, and I decided to stretch out like a diva because I had just conquered the road."

Mom: Rhonda K. Davis
Daughter: Roxanne Clark
Era: 1982, Los Angeles, California

"I have always had an extreme love of cars," says Rhonda. "I was in my
very early twenties in this photo. My car was a 1974 Camaro, and it was
my love. When I bought it, it was average looking, but I felt it had
potential. I didn't have a lot of money, but I invested in it over time,
including low-profile tires, customized paint, tinted windows, rims. I
had power, speed, and an awesome-looking car."

The black silk dress wasn't bad either, though daughter Roxanne notes:
"It was one of her most conservative outfits."

Mom: Kathy Hall
Daughter: Anna Carollo
Era: Circa 1974

"I've often told people that there's
no way I could ever be as cool as
my mom," says Anna, "and this photo
serves as a great example. She owned
and rode many motorcycles through
the years (mostly BMWs and Hondas),
picked up and moved to the middle
of nowhere in Maine for a while,
and was a total babe to boot."

Mom: Bruni Jaeger
Niece: Susan Hasten
Era: 1974

Nothing got between Bruni
and her Honda. Not even big
hair. "My mom's sister had
three kids when she started
riding a motorcycle," says
Susan. "Hidden underneath
the helmet was her wicked-
black beehive hairstyle,
in addition to the heavy
drawn-on eyebrows and
black eyeliner."

Mom: Kimalyn Louise Hatton
Daughter: Ruby Roberts
Era: 1982

"The car was a gift from my dad's friend, since my mom didn't have a car," says Ruby. "It was very ratty when she got it, but it ran well. This picture was taken after she had it painted and fixed up. They got all dressed up and drove it to a seafood restaurant across the river, taking the ferry and showing it off." Kimalyn, who was pregnant with Ruby at the time, still refers to that blue punch-buggy as her "baby."

THE LIFE OF THE PARTY

Some people just know how to get down. Others even made it their business. Regardless of the venue—a basement, a nightclub, or an office party—these were mothers everyone was talking about.

Mom: Sofia Oganezov
Daughter: Dasha Oganezov
Era: 1967, Moscow

"At that time, Western music was prohibited in the USSR, you had to go to an underground club or a house party to 'do the twist,'" says Dasha. "Clothing, even something as classic as a white shirt and pencil skirt, was hard to come by, so stylish girls like my mom relied on their own, their mothers', and their sisters' sewing skills to come up with unique designs. This particular outfit was handmade by my grandma."

Mom: Julie Wood
Daughter: Jennifer Lawson
Era: 1976, California

One Halloween in the '70s, Jennifer Lawson's brother, David, dressed as a cross between Superman and Zorro. Jennifer was either a devil or Little Red Riding Hood. But there was no question about what her mom, Julie, was: beer. "My mom was pretty wild when she was young, so it doesn't surprise me she showed up to work as a bank teller dressed as a beer can. I'm still wondering why I don't seem to have a costume," says Jennifer.

Mom: Gertrude Sofman
Daughter: Elizabeth Sofman
Era: 1975, Morristown, New Jersey

"This homemade butterfly getup was her Halloween costume," says Elizabeth of her mother. "She also got a butterfly tattoo the year before, when she was eighteen. So when I was nineteen, she took me to a tattoo parlor, and I got a replica of her butterfly. Total mother-daughter moment."

Mom: Carnetta Jones Turek
Daughter: Hana Turek
Era: 1974, Oakland, California

Before she was Hana's mom, Carnetta (at right)
was a Catholic schoolgirl with a wild streak.
"All of us Catholic-school girls had to wear
a uniform—a checkered green skirt with a white
Peter Pan collared shirt. We were desperate to
stand out and look different. So when we had
free-dress day, we dressed in our individual
styles. My style was punctuated with big hoop
earrings and a jean scarf tied into a bun on
the back of my head," remembers Carnetta.

The photo in the car was taken on a Friday
after school, when the girls had changed out
of their uniforms and into their trouble-
stirring stitches. "We loaded up in the car
and then waited at a liquor store to get an
adult to buy us beer. Then we drove up to our
secret spot where we'd drink."

The night started off as planned, blasting
Laura Nyro on the eight-track and kicking
back cold ones. Around midnight, the girls
were ready to go home. "That's when the car
wouldn't start," Carnetta recalls. "So we all
huddled arm and arm and walked under the light
of the moon." They finally found a phone booth
and called for help, also known as parents.
It didn't go over well. "We cried after our
parents grounded us. We were scared straight
for at least a month."

Carnetta in the car ready for adventure.

photos courtesy of Carnetta Turek and Sonja Tate

In her other high school uniform, designed for rabble-rousing.

Mom: Natasza Dimmock
Daughter: Jessica Dimmock
Era: 1963, Brooklyn, New York

Teenaged Natasza at a sweet sixteen,
puffs on a smoke while the chaperones
have turned their backs.

photo by Larry Wolfinsohn, courtesy of the Wolfinsohn family

The Sporty Two-Piece

Mom: Susan Wolfinsohn
Son: Ben Wolfinsohn
Era: Late 1970s, Wisconsin

The Farrah

Mom: K. C. Cousins
Daughter: Kelly Cousins
Era: Late 1970s, South Carolina

In 1976, K. C. wore this green spaghetti-strap one-piece on her honeymoon. That same year, Farrah Fawcett wore the suit in red and posed for a photograph that would kick-start puberty for preteen boys around the country.

The Belted Bikini

Mom: Barbara Schwartz
Daughter: Lara D'Agostino
Era: 1966, New York

The Belted Beacher

Mom: Suzanne Kovacs
Daughter: Anne-Marie Kovacs
Era: 1967, Quebec, Canada

The Hybrid

Mom: Joan Davisson
Daughter: Leslie Davisson
Destination: Hawaii
Era: 1973

"The belt is bigger than those shorts," says Joan, who worked as a high school teacher when her new husband whisked her away to Hawaii. Accessories were just her thing, even on the tropical beaches. "Her outfits are ensembles—with splashes of color, artisan jewelry, interesting textures, and a little sparkle," says Leslie. "Being only 5 foot, 1 inch, I thought she dressed this way to stand out because she was short." But Joan says her height is irrelevant. "I just want to be remembered."

The Designer Bikini

Mom: Patricia Malesardi
Daughter: Paula Hansen
Era: Late 1960s, New York

As a model for a bikini company, Patricia sampled
the finest lingerie cum swimwear on the market.

scrapbook:
MAUREEN, THE BATHING BEAUTY

IN THE EARLY 1950s, Maureen Hart left her job at Harrods and her family in England to sail across the world with her husband and two-year-old daughter, Deborah. Making a home in the Fijian Islands, Deborah Hart spent her childhood eating mangoes and sugar cane. Maureen, however, spent her time cultivating designs for swimsuits. In the '50s, exotic swimwear was still in its infancy. But Maureen wasn't afraid to experiment with form, texture, and fabric—or lack there of.

"My mother made everything—including swim-suits. She was one of the first to don a bikini at the sailing club in Fiji. She used to write and ask my grandmother to send her patterns, mainly Vogue and McCall's. She also adapted designs and patterns herself because, on the island, things were quite difficult to get."

"I have a sewing book from Vogue in the 1950s with patterns and fashion pictures that belonged to my mom. I loved the clothes she made me. I was always getting new dresses and pantsuits. My father, who worked at the airport in Fiji, told me that the American wives of his coworkers would ask my mom to make things for them."

"Sometimes on the weekend, Mom and Dad would sail off to one of the many deserted islands around Fiji. We lived in Fiji for five years until my mother became quite ill. They decided to come back to England so her family could spend some time with her. In her short married life, she certainly saw the world."

THE ZOOKEEPERS

Before the national nightmare of tiny toy dogs in Chanel booties, people just had normal dogs and cats. But they also had some really weird pets.

Mom: Claire Pearl Wodlinger Murray
Granddaughter: Angela Pastor
Era: 1938, Vancouver Island,
  British Columbia, Canada
Pet: Gerbil

"My grandmother was twenty years old at the time of this photo," says Angela. "Her husband was a logger, and they rented a cabin in the middle of the woods from a man named Cougar Lee, who lived there with his family and hunted cougars—hence the nickname. Since her husband was away all week working, my grandma spent all her time with Cougar Lee who taught her to hunt deer, grouse, lay traps, and grow her own food. She also had a dog and a cat for company—and that little gerbil or mouse, although no one in my family knows where it came from. It was possibly a wild animal she found out there. I can't imagine living like that and still managing to look so incredibly stylish, but that was Claire."

Mom: Janet Marshall
Daughter: Alice Marshall
Era: 1961, Hastings, England
Pet: Monkey

"This has always been my favorite picture of my mom," says Alice Marshall. "She's fifteen and holding her little sister and, inexplicably, a monkey."

Mom: Marilyn Weiss
Daughter: Piper Weiss
Era: 1960s Greenwhich Village, New York
Pet: Parrot

"My mom's bird was the perfect party trick. And it added a splash of color to anything she wore. The little bugger fared better than my father's parakeet, who famously died when it landed in a boiling pot of soup."

4

The Originals:
From the People Who Brought You Everything You Wear Now

Some people are born trendsetters. Before the form-fitting hoodie hit the celebrity circuit, Mrs. Orzolek wore it on a sunny day in Seoul. And before thousands of women applied for high-powered media jobs in Diane Von Furstenberg wrap dresses, Mrs. Berman tied one on with a pair of oversized sunglasses. It's a fact that the garment industry was more diverse in past decades and that home sewing machines were a staple in households. But beyond all that, some women just knew what styles would endure, even before they hit the mainstream.

THE ORIGINAL HIPSTERS

American Apparel did not invent sportswear. Moms did. These women ushered bright colors, leg warmers, high-waisted jeans, and terry cloth into existence (with a little help from Jane Fonda).

Mom: Kathy Raupp
Daughter: Aimee Raupp
Era: Early 1980s, New Jersey
Originated: Aerobics gear

Aimee's mother was an aerobics teacher. As if you couldn't tell. Before cardio-boxing and boot-cut yoga pants—the look was a leotard, the accessory was a sweatband, and the motto was "Take no prisoners."

"I used to love to go to classes with my mom," says Aimee. "She was always the best dressed. Back then she was teaching for Jackie Sorenson. It was the original aerobic cult: instructors had to weigh in, and, if they didn't make weight, they couldn't teach classes that week." The tradeoff was the kind of body that could work spandex as evening apparel. "She loved to wear her workout outfit after class. She wouldn't even shower; she'd just hit the town."

Mom: Karen Ann Willert
Daughter: Kathy Willert
Era: 1981, California
Originated: Velour as evening wear

Mom: Linda Garces
Daughter: Mariana Garces
Era: 1978, New Hampshire
Originated: Mary Kate Olsen's eyewear

Mom: Janet McQuarrie
Daughter: Ryann McQuarrie-Salik
Era: 1980s, Canada
Originated: The striped T-shirt of the hot pink variety

Mom, 1964

Mom: Letitia Nichols
Daughter: Emily Nichols
Era: 1964, Upstate New York
Originated: Fitted plaid shirts

"There is a bit of mystery
surrounding who took this
picture," says Emily. "We
know my mom was nineteen and
a stylish college student at
Niagara University. Written
on the front of the photo is
"Mom, 1964." Written on the
back is: "I'm keeping all
the rest for myself."

my mom,
THE TRENDSETTER

An interview with Karen O and Munja Orzolek

AS LEAD SINGER OF THE BAND THE YEAH YEAH YEAHS, KAREN O is a trendsetter. She has propelled small designers into the fashion stratosphere and spurred on thousands of female fans to covet primary colors, stretch dresses, and bangs. Blinding black bangs. But even Karen got her inspiration from somewhere. Namely, her mom—Munja Orzolek.

Where was this photo taken?

KAREN: In Seoul in 1976, to run in a catalog for my father's outerwear manufacturing company. She was a young mother living in Seoul, recently married to my dad, who was a broke Polish American guy, much to her family's disapproval. Marriage to Westerners was frowned on in those days, so in this sense she was very rebellious for a woman living in '70s Korea.

What makes your mom's style individual?

KAREN: My mom has been called the Korean Audrey Hepburn, but instead of pearls around her neck, it's a sculptural Marni necklace, and a little black dress by McQueen. I should also mention that she rarely pays full price for anything.

MUNJA: I loved miniskirts and dresses accessorized with hip-slung belts. Other big favorites were bell-bottom pants with platform shoes and head scarves. It's all about the clean and chic styles with a little twist. I've always tried to personalize and reinterpret the fashion trends so I won't get caught wearing the same outfit as another person in the room.

Was there a time when you didn't share the same fashion sensibilities?

MUNJA: Karen's favorite high-school style invited my nagging. The "Grunge" look: sloppy layers; floor-sweeping, frayed hem; and clothes worn inside out.

KAREN: We didn't see eye to eye almost entirely throughout high school. I shopped at thrift stores for corduroy pants and grandma sweaters in my efforts to be an "alterna-hippie." I remember my mom would knock on my door and give me a friendly reminder: "You know, Karen, grunge is out." I guess it had been in season on catwalks for a brief moment in time. That used to really piss me off, like she SO doesn't get me.

How has your mom's style then informed what you wear on stage?

KAREN: Her refined style has aided in refining my style. I must subconsciously emulate her edgy elegance as I become a woman. I'm probably a bit more quirky than she's ever been, though, and will probably get more so as time passes.

photo by Kim Chong Su

THE ORIGINAL DRESS EXPERIENCE

No item of clothing better exemplifies an era than a dress. It's a front-and-center reflection of popular culture, counterculture, and the wearer's navigation of both.

The Bubble Dress

Mom: Barbara Schwartz
Daughter: Lara D'Agostino
Era: 1960, New York

"We called this a bubble dress, and I wore it to my high-school dance," says Barbara. "My date, of course, was the captain of the football team."

The Weekend Adventure Dress

Mom: Kathleen Hewitt
Daughter: Kristen Hewitt
Era: 1967, Santa Cruz Mountains

Lady in Red

Mom: May Wong
Daughter: Lisa Wong Jackson
Era: Late 1960s

The Trompe L'Oeil

Mom: Jeanne Albert
Daughter: Madeleine Berenson
· Era: 1954, Boardman, Ohio

"That picture was taken in the backyard of the home where I was born and raised," remembers Jeanne. "I had come home from New York City to tell my parents about this wonderful man I had met in New York whom I was going to marry. I hoped they would love him as much as I did and that they would be fully in favor of this marriage. None of us had the money to arrange any meeting before we got married. My future husband was finishing up his graduate school work at New York University—broke as any college student could be in those days. I had no travel money since I was earning the fantastic sum of $54 per week," says Jeanne, who was working as a researcher at *Time* magazine. "Very frugal living made it possible for me to purchase that dress I was wearing from Saks Fifth Avenue—on sale. It was a knit dress that would travel well, pack in a suitcase, and not need ironing—just the thing to wear on a visit home to announce the most important decision of my life."

Despite her struggle to pay for the dress, this was one of the few times Jeanne would ever wear it. "The first day I wore it to work at *Time*,

my supervisor pulled me aside and advised me that it was not really an appropriate outfit for work—the buttons were badly placed. I never felt comfortable wearing it any place after that," says Jeanne.

The dress and the wistful image of her young mother have captivated daughter Madeleine. "I am fascinated by this picture of my mother, because in it she is someone I don't know. She and my father had eight children," says Madeleine. "As far back as I can remember, she never bought anything for herself—she even dressed in my father's old clothes and cut her own hair. We had money, too, so it had nothing to do with what we could afford. I think she just disappeared into becoming what the people around her needed, and ended up regarding self-deprivation as a virtue, and anything related to fashion or beauty as a wasteful, selfish vice. Maybe it was easier that way. But in this picture, she looks as glamorous as Leslie Caron, brimming with just as much girlish confidence. She looks like she knows exactly how beautiful she is, which makes my heart ache."

The Bib

Mom: Linda Hand
Daughter: Autumn Hand
Era: 1975, Ohio

The Diva Gowns

Mom: Faith Winthrop
Daughter: Erika Lenkert
Era: 1950s

For a professional jazz singer, finding your look was almost as important as finding your voice. "What I wore depended on where I was. As the house singer for the San Francisco jazz club, the Hungry I, in 1955 to 1957, I wore cashmere outfits, Japanese silk skirts, and tops with an obi sash. But I dressed up when I performed in concert venues," says Faith, who opened for Billie Holiday in 1954.

One particular gold-sequined dress, which she wore for promotional pictures, was designed by critical fashion legend Mr. Blackwell. "I

bought it in Westwood Village in Los Angeles in 1956 or 1957. It was on hold for Dorothy Lamour. They told me to come back the following week, and if Dorothy Lamour couldn't fit into it, it was mine. So I came back. I think it cost about $75. That was money then." It was well worth it. Her daughter inherited the gold-sequined gown and wore it to a party a couple of years ago. "She's got a closet full of fancy stuff for me. Caribou, leather, cashmere—you name it," says Erika.

my mom,
THE DESIGNER LABEL ICON

IN HER EARLY TWENTIES, BROOKE BERMAN STARTED RAIDING her mother's closet. "A pair of Krizia quilted paisley pants stand out in my memory and this one particular Gucci suede skirt from 1973," she says.

A fashion publicist by trade, Marilyn Lucas Berman had a closet that could rival Anna Wintour, or, in Brooke's own words, Imelda Marcos. "In 2004, my mom, who suffered from severe diabetes, had her leg amputated. So she tried to give her shoes to me. This was a woman with a closet full of designer shoes in perfect condition, each pair stored in the box it came in—Chanel, Walter Steiger, Charles Jourdan."

When the disease took Marilyn's life in 2007, Brooke turned to her mother's closet for solace. "I wear my mother's sunglasses every day—I had my own prescription lenses put in—and a gold locket I found in her jewelry box," says Brooke, a playwright and author. "As for the hand-me-downs, they are of two categories: the really fabulous stuff—anything Vuitton, anything Gucci—and then, the really basic, non-designer stuff. For instance, I could wear my mom's socks or her yellow Gap slicker and feel close to her through the grieving process, as if she and I were having a conversation as her soul was letting go of this life, getting ready to move on."

THE ORIGINAL PHOTO MAGNETS

In the age of Polaroid and Kodak film, one shot was all our mothers had. Many times this resulted in stiff portraits and formal poses. But some women were naturals in front of the camera, even with the high price of film.

photo courtesy of the Odeh family

Mom: Judith Ann Reeves Odeh
Daughter: Stephanie Odeh
Era: 1967, California

"My father had taken my mother to the pier in Long Beach specifically to take her picture, which he would send back home to his mother, sister, and brother in Jordan," says Stephanie. "My mother said my father wanted to introduce the family 'to the young lady he was going to marry.' It was a success. They wed two months later.

Mom: Eileen Wilson
Granddaughter: Melissa McLaughlin
Era: 1966, Massachusetts

The ripped jean shorts are partially covered by grass. But for
Melissa, this photo of her grandmother isn't about the clothes.
"I always think of it as her modeling picture: she's posed and put
together, without even trying," she says. "She was relaxing, and
my grandfather, who was supposed to be watching his children play,
instead turned the camera on her. So this is just her effortless,
innate elegance."

Mom: Jeanne Paige
Daughter: Jackie Deller
Era: Late 1960s

"I really love this photo," says Jackie. "It was taken by
my dad when they were out walking. It looks like it could
be used for a fashion spread in a magazine, but it was
just another day of looking cool for my mom."

Mom: Amy Teplin Post
Daughter: Wallis Post
Era: 1971, New York City

"My mom was a fashion editor at a menswear magazine in New York. She had just been given her own column, so they did a photo shoot to have some glamour pics taken, including this one," says Wallis. "A number of months before the shoot, she saw this fabric that she loved in London. When she had enough money, she worked with a tailor to design the outfit."

THE MENSWEAR ORIGINALS

In the '80s, Secret deodorant had the tagline "Made for a man, but PH balanced for a woman." It was a bad campaign. No one really knew or cared what PH was. But the idea that products designed for men are better on women holds true. Regardless of sweat glands. Amelia Earhart and Katharine Hepburn knew that a long time ago. So did a few moms who picked up a fedora at a thrift store or a blazer from their son's closet and thought, "Wait a minute. . . ." It's a lightbulb moment. And regardless of the era, it's always a look PH balanced for fashion risk takers.

photo by Larry Wolfinsohn, courtesy of the Wolfinsohn family

Mom: Susan Wolfinsohn
Son: Ben Wolfinsohn
Era: 1970s and 1980s, the Midwest

Ben's mother never dressed like other women . . . not even in high school. "She actually wanted to wear a tux to the prom," says Ben. As a teenager in Chicago, most of her clothing was handmade. She would spend Saturdays picking out patterns and material for pleated skirts and sweaters, which her mother would then construct by hand. Susan's one request: Nothing frilly. "She was always a minimalist. She shunned flowers and jewelry," says Ben.

Mom: Patricia Malesardi
Daughter: Paula Hansen
Era: Late 1960s, New York City

For Patricia, modeling for a leather goods company was more than a job. It was
an opportunity to keep the clothes. The suede leather aviator-inspired coat was
part of the payment. So was a matching leather dress underneath the coat and the
leather turban on her head. Eventually Patricia had to pay it forward. "I'm now
the proud owner," says Paula.

Mom: Laura Bobey
Son: John Bobey
Era: 1970s, Upstate New York

Mom: Joy Robertson
Daughter: Emily Materick
Era: 1970, Toronto, Canada

my mom,
THE MODEL

Interview with John Buffalo Mailer, son of Norris Church Mailer

IN 1969, NORRIS CHURCH MAILER WAS MODELING CHECKERED prairie dresses. Six years later, she was posing for the camera in sequined gowns. Her glamour ratcheted up along with her profile when she met writer Norman Mailer in 1975 at a party in her native state of Arkansas. Soon after, the aspiring writer moved to New York, signed with Wilhelmina modeling agency, and became Norman's sixth and final wife. In 1978, she gave birth to their son John Buffalo Mailer.

As a young boy, John was less interested in his mother's—by then coveted—fashion sense, than by its powerful effect on people. John, now a writer and actor, remembers the year she was labeled by one magazine "most coveted person to sit next to at a dinner party." But John always got first dibs on the seat.

When did you realize your mother was stylish?

When I was young, she used to walk me to school, and the other boys would always run to catch up with us but seemed more interested in talking to my mom than to me. I figured it must have something to do with her style. I'm incredibly proud to have a mother who knows how to let her own light shine. I have always been of the belief that when you allow yourself to shine as bright as you know you can and do not hold yourself back for fear of intimidating other people, you unconsciously give those others the permission to do the same. I believe this is one of the many reasons people tend to fall in love with my mom upon meeting her; they feel their most beautiful when she is around them.

Right: A 1969 modeling shot for the Log Cabin Democrat in Arkansas. "It was one of the pictures I sent to Eileen Ford when I made the effort to come to New York and be a model," remembers Norris Mailer. "She was unimpressed. I gave up my dream of being a model, and didn't think about it again until I moved to New York in 1975 and signed with Wilhelmina."

Did you observe any of her beauty rituals as a kid?

When we were young, my brother and I would hang out with her and talk about where she was going and who she was going to be talking to at dinner while she was putting on her makeup and blow-drying her hair. It felt almost like she was a Roman gladiator getting prepared to enter the arena and conquer whatever challenge would be placed in front of her. My mother has the ability to make most things seem like an adventure.

Is there a lesson you could extract from her style?

For me, style has always been about wearing what fits your character, what is true to your identity. My mom never spent a ridiculous amount on clothes. In fact she prides herself on not spending a lot on clothes and still looking like she just stepped out of the pages of a magazine. I can't pretend to be as well put together as my mother. But I did take the notion that it doesn't matter how much a shirt costs; it matters whether it fits in the metaphorical sense. For that I am grateful.

photo by Bill Ward

A modeling test photo in New York in 1976.

photos by Will Ryan

Right: Another test photo from the same shoot. "That black-and-gold sequin dress and matching shoes were a Christmas gift from Norman," says Norris. "The dress was from the '30s, I think; he got it at a wonderful vintage store in SoHo called Harriet Love that he knew I liked, and it was a total surprise. I wore it only a couple of times; it was so fragile. The last time was on Halloween one year, when I dressed up as a Jean Harlow kind of movie star, complete with platinum wig. I have the dress and shoes still, carefully wrapped in tissue."

5

Going to the Chapel:
The Only Dress That Ever Mattered

The wedding-day photo is the first evidence that our mothers had a life before us. At a glance, this much we knew: they got dressed up, they were beautiful, and—at least for one day—they were in love. Sometimes due to fog-swept backgrounds and '70s photo technology, it also seems they held the ceremony on the set of a sitcom dream sequence. Looking through the wedding album as an adult, you can learn a lot about Mom. The photos are a catalog of the choices she made—from the dress to the groom.

There are only a few pictures of my parents' wedding in existence. "The photographer was stoned," says my mom, Marilyn, who was twenty-five the day she wed. "I wanted someone artsy and creative, but this guy forgot to turn the flash on."

"Maybe it was our fault—maybe he lit up when he walked into the rabbi's study and saw our crazy family," she says. It's not entirely a joke. That day there were fights between family members and sneering comments from jealous wives of exes. The day was far from perfect. The gown, however, was a home run. A snow-white angora sweater dress with pearl buttons and bell princess sleeves is, to this day, unlike any I've ever seen. It's the kind of outfit you want to sleep in. Not exactly something you expect out of a wedding dress.

"I bought it at Saks on my lunch break when I working at an ad agency," says my mom, who made her own veil with material found in the notion district on the west side of Manhattan. "It wasn't a wedding dress because I really didn't have a wedding."

My parents, Marilyn and Monroe (yes, you read correctly) met in the Bahamas on an overbooked flight and were engaged three months later. They had two things in common—their Alma Mater, Forest Hills High School, and broken engagements. Both had canceled massive weddings with exes. "You learn things about your partner when you're planning a big wedding that you don't necessarily like," Marilyn says.

So, when my parents were married in Queens on November 22, 1970, the choice was clear: a small ceremony in the rabbi's study and then a bagels-and-lox brunch at my grandma's house on the other side of Queens Boulevard. By noon they were on a plane to Venezuela for their honeymoon. But the dress, wrapped in plastic, stayed in Queens. It also stayed on all the guests' clothing.

"Everyone was walking around with white fluff from the dress," says my mom who celebrates her fortieth anniversary with my father this year. "If you hugged me, you left with a little piece of me."

CLASSIC GLAMOUR

Decades may dictate bridal looks, but some dresses are always in fashion. The princess crinoline, the mile-long bustle, the lace veil flowing over-head, are items passed on in form and in practice by our great-grandmothers. For the bride, they always feel brand new.

Mom: Barbara Waxler
Daughter: Caroline Waxler
Era: 1964, New York City

"The photo was taken about three to four weeks before the wedding, at a photographer's studio. It ended up running in the *New York Times*," says Caroline. "My mom's sister, comedienne Joan Rivers, was the matron of honor. Her gift was to pay for a makeup artist to do my mom's face for the photos." With or without makeup, Barbara beamed. At twenty-seven, she had met her future husband Edward at Bellvue. "Not the mental institution part," clarifies Caroline. He was a med student; she was volunteering at the hospital. Their wedding was a four-day extravaganza that began at city hall, and ended at her parents' house in Larchmont. She wore the dress to all—a total of three receptions—without even so much as a red wine stain. It's a good thing, too, because Barbara's dress was a real find: "Two hundred dollars, from Henri Bendel's," says Barbara. "It was reduced from $400 because it was used in a show."

Daughter: Colleen Kluttz
Era: 1970s

At twenty-six, Polly was considered an old bride. By then, she was responsible
for making her own living and buying her own wedding dress—it cost her $50.

"I love that Mom didn't care that things weren't perfect," says Colleen.

Only eight months prior, Polly had met her groom on a blind date, and here they
were rushing to sign a contract. It's one they still haven't broken. "Recently
my mom said, 'I just wanted to get married. I mean, I loved your father, but not
like I do now.'"

Mom: Carol Moss
Daughter: Jenny Moss
Date: 1963, Wimbledon, England

The daughter of a cabbie and a sales clerk, Carol Moss's background was far more modest than her husband's. But for her wedding day, she stepped into the role of his princess, with a parchment silk dress and tiara veil from a London department store. Carol, then an employee at the *London Daily Mirror*, had met her groom, a wealthy antiques dealer, on the tennis courts. "Her trademark look was large sunglasses and baker boy caps," says Jenny. "She really embraced the '60s style of London and loved shopping."

Mom: Victoria Littleton Tucker
Daughter: Jane Borden
Era: 1969, Danville, Virginia

The first dress Victoria tried on at Montaldos, a chain of boutiques for women in the South, was THE one. "It was the most beautiful dress I have ever seen. Very Jackie O." The lace veil was a family heirloom from Brussels and one that every Tucker woman would walk down the aisle wearing.

Mom: Letitia Nichols
Daughter: Emily Nichols
Era: 1966, Niagara Falls, New York

"My mom's (pictured with her father) sense of style was a combination
of classic and fashionable. She knew what looked good on her, and I never
recall her being under- or overdressed for an event; she had an internal
fashion barometer."

Letitia lived by a few fashion credos she applied readily on her wedding
day: "She believed you should always wear a camisole—even under a camisole,"
remembers Emily. "Also, special occasions require special clothes, and
finally you can't teach someone good tastes. It has to come naturally."
Lucky for Letitia, it did.

my mom,
THE ICONIC BRIDE

An Interview with Chloe Sevigny

CHLOE SEVIGNY CAN DRESS HERSELF. THIS MAY BE AN unremarkable statement for the average person, but for a celebrity whose career hinges on being the most magnetic person in the room, it's a trade skill. One that doesn't come from front-row seats at runway shows, or personal stylists, but from bloodlines. One look at Chloe's mother Janine Sevigny on her wedding day, and it's obvious: style is genetic.

When did your parents get married?

My mother, Janine, and my father, David, were married in the morning on November 24, 1966, in Philadelphia. They were in their mid-twenties and had fallen in love at first sight. My father was serving in the Marine Corps and was home on leave the day they were married.

What was she wearing?

She wore a white minidress and headpiece from Saks in New York. Her bridesmaids—her sisters—wore Pucci dresses. She wore white gloves and had a simple bouquet of gardenias.

What is it about her look that captivates you?

My mom's bridal look is so classic and simple and ethereal. This look epitomizes my mother to me: a modern angel whose beauty and kindness shines so bright she doesn't need any frills. If her dress were still around, I would have probably worn it to bits already.

Did you always share a similar sense of style?

In high school, I wore all her old dresses including one of her prom dresses to my prom. I do still have one of the Puccis.

Some time capsules are made of lace. These bridal dresses will transport you to the altars of fashion in decades past.

Mom: Mary Carter
Daughter: Lucy Carter
Era: Early 1970s, England

Part rock star, part priestess—there is something distinctly Marianne Faithfull about Mary's whimsical, willowy wedding dress. Blame it on Ossie Clark, captain of swinging '60s London fashion, who designed the dress. He also designed costumes for Faithfull and her paramour, Mick Jagger.

Mom: Ginny Green
Daughter: Ryan Green
Era: 1974, Massachusetts

Ryan Green's mom recycled a sundress
she wore to her sister's wedding. Her
"something new" was the choker. It
probably cost more than the wedding
itself.

"My parents met in college in November
of 1969 driving down to an antiwar march
in Washington," says Ryan. "Their wedding
was in my grandparents' backyard, and my
dad's brother, a minister, officiated."

Mom: Esther Rotter
Daughter: Jess Rotter
Era: 1977, Long Island, New York

"It's gorgeous 1970s surreal foreshadowing at its best. My mother examining
her ring and anticipating the rest of her life while my father's godlike
profile looms large," says Jess. "My mom's choice of bright baby-blue eye-
shadow is a bit of an eyebrow raiser for me. But I am really into her
sweet wispy feather hair action."

PHOTO SHAKIB TEHRAN

MAR. 1967

Mom: Carol Belanger
Daughter: Victoria Belanger
Era: 1973, New Jersey

"My mother made her own wedding dress to match my father's rented powder blue, ruffled tux," says Victoria. "She had to dye the lacy parts of the dress blue herself, as the lace that she liked only came in white. She also made all the dresses for her bridesmaids."

It was a bold move, but love drives you to do crazy things. Like skip your own wedding party—at your own apartment. "They had a bathtub filled with ice and booze at their place for their friends," says Victoria. "But they went straight to the hotel."

Mom: Ronda Crossett Provost
Daughter: Devon Geiger
Era: 1965, Tehran, Iran

Ronda had been working in the Peace Corps in Iran when she met her husband. "That experience made her concentrate more on comfort and necessity when it came to style," says Devon. Her wedding at the consulate was an exception. A lamb's wool pillbox hat topped off a bridal look that could be matched only by a certain First Lady.

Mom: Desanka Loncar Nikolic
Daughter: Jana Orsolic
Era: 1976, Belgrade, Serbia

Leather was big in the '70s. And some of the most innovative designs
using the material came from the Belgrade area. A Yugoslav designer
named Mirjana Maric was known for transforming high-quality leather
into women's suits, jackets, pocketbooks, and, yes, wedding dresses.
The leather was stippled to soften the fabric. Belgrade-native Desanka
modeled a Maric original on her big day. "The dress was made of thin
white leather," says Jana. "She used to say that it was so comfy."

Mom: Ellen Maxwell
Daughter: Elsbeth Maxwell
Era: 1976, Holland

Ellen's dress was made from scratch
with the help of her mother-in-law.
The thick lining, which her groom's
mother insisted on for propriety,
left her with memories of being
sweltering hot. Her shoes weren't
exactly comfortable, either. "They
were vintage—my mother's—a size
too big, and I had hand-painted
them white especially for the
occasion," says Ellen. "My husband-to-be had glued the dodgy
heel on, but it came off half
way through the day."

Mom: Judy Posch
Daughter: Brooke Posch
Era: 1973, Long Island

In one year, Judy went from bridesmaid to bride. "At that time she was a twenty-three-year-old secretary living in New York City, when she met my dad at a wedding," says Brooke.

"We were partners in the bridal party," explains Judy. "As we were walking up the stairs to be introduced along with the bride to the entire wedding party, Bob stepped on the back of my dress and it tore right at the seam from under my breast to the middle of my back. I was suddenly naked and screamed out a profanity. I ran into the ladies room and borrowed a needle and thread from the coat clerk and sat there on the toilet bowl, in my birthday suit, sewing the dress. They had to stop the reception for me. The next week Bob and I started to date."

For her wedding the following year, Judy trimmed her own dress in yellow to match her bridesmaids—a nod in part to the bridesmaid's dress that brought them together.

my mom,
THE BRIDE AGAIN

PATRICK MAHONEY WAS TWELVE WHEN HIS MOTHER MARRIED for the sixth time. It was early spring of 1968, and a few days before, he'd accompanied his mom, Phyllis, to local shops in search of a dress for the occasion. "She'd been married so many times; she didn't want a traditional wedding dress."

Patrick waited outside the dressing room at a Long Beach boutique as his mother tried on dress after dress. He was there to provide his opinion as much as he was there to marvel at her. "Maybe it was because I was a gay boy or because we had been through so much, but I was fascinated by how she put herself together," says Patrick. To add to her bridal look, she bought gold shoes and a purse to match. "That was her rule, the shoes and purses always had to match." It was a delicate balance, choosing an outfit for your sixth wedding. Patrick, though still a child, understood.

When he was born in 1955, Phyllis had already been widowed by her first husband (a fighter pilot), had another son, moved to Japan, then moved to Mexico City, and returned to the States to meet a new husband, Patrick's father.

"I knew she'd been married a lot, but when I pulled out her papers after she passed away it really hit me—there was a huge stack of marriage licenses. But Mom was always very careful about my brother and me—she never married guys that did us harm. They were all trying to be healthy, responsible people."

In 1968, Phyllis, by then a recovering alcoholic and sober counselor, met her sixth husband, Johnny Cowman, at an AA meeting. He had just gotten out of prison and wanted to turn his life around. "At the end of the meetings, they stand in circles and say the Lord's Prayer, and he said my mom made a pass at him." Besides their sobriety, Phyllis and Johnny shared a mutual appreciation for clothing and the care of them. Johnny owned a dry-cleaning business in Long Beach, and Patrick and Phyllis joined him in running it.

"I learned about care of fabrics, what goes together and what doesn't." He also learned to look at clothing in a new way. "Long Beach was populated with a lot of retired people then. For that generation, if you were doing well, you expressed it by how you dressed. While their retirement was running out, they spent money to have their forty-year-old clothes dry-cleaned. Even if they never wore them, they were the last remnants of who they were and what they had earned. I learned how hard it is for most people to let go of that."

Letting go was a skill Patrick most admired in his mom. After years of overcoming addiction and broken marriages, Phyllis knew better than to let her past or her past outfits define her future choices. "She didn't need to hold onto things," says Patrick. "A year after her marriage, Mom gave away the gold dress she wore at the wedding." Johnny, her sixth and final husband, she kept.

Patrick throws rice at his mother and her new husband as they leave the church.

Phyllis's gold wedding dress for her sixth walk down the aisle.

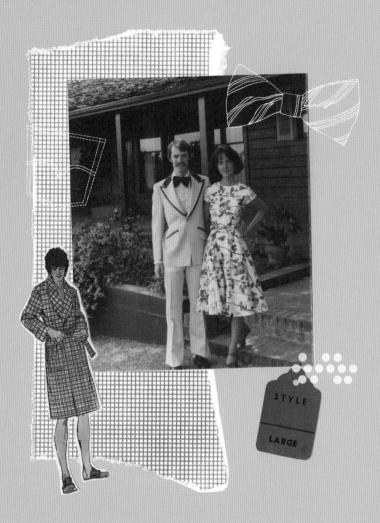

STYLE

LARGE

>>>>>>>> 6 <<<<<<<<

Lucky Dads:
Fashion for Better or for Worse

A 1955 issue of *Housekeeping Monthly* offered a piece of advice for young women hoping to keep their husbands' interest:

Touch up your makeup, put a ribbon in your hair and be fresh-looking.

Sure. Now meet the mothers in this chapter. Keeping a man's rapt attention was not an issue. And it had nothing to do with any ribbon.

The Couple: Linda and Wilf Sandl
Daughter: Andrea Sandl
Era: 1977
The Look: White disco suits

"My parents were on their way to the airport for their honeymoon in Hawaii," says Andrea. "So, not only are they totally rocking in the three-piece pantsuits, but this picture is a lovely example of the days when people actually dressed up to travel."

The Couple: Gail and Alan Horlick
Daughter: Rachel Horlick
Era: 1970s
The Look: Partners in Plaid

The Couple: Patsy and Terry Moore
Daughter: Reese Moore
Era: 1970s
The Look: Happy Campers

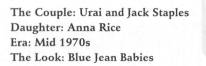

The Couple: Urai and Jack Staples
Daughter: Anna Rice
Era: Mid 1970s
The Look: Blue Jean Babies

"She met my dad in Bangkok in early 1975 when she was
managing a building. He was her tenant," says Anna. "At the
time she was a single mom who had backed out of an arranged
marriage, and he was stationed in the army. They were married
after only three months."

FIERCE COMPETITION

Dads will try, and some try too hard, but they can't outshine their women.

The Couple: Janet and Brian McQuarrie
Daughter: Ryann McQuarrie-Salik
Era: Late 1970s, Canada

The couple that shops together, stays together. Even if the guy picks out a white suit. For the 1977 Valentine's Day dance at the University of Victoria, the new couple decided to hunt for their outfits together. "My dad picked out my mom's dress. She tried it on for him, and he bought it for her on the spot," says daughter Ryann.

Janet had no say in Brian's disco suit. It was just the beginning of a life of Brian's rowdy fashion choices: "The late 1970s were a tumultuous time style-wise. Some days my dad's denim cutoffs were shorter than my mom's, but he always knew when to take a step back and really let her shine."

The Couple: Joe and Harriett Banner
Daughter: Chrissa Banner
Era: Early 1970s

"Thanksgiving dinner, the year before I was born," says Chrissa. "I love the simple elegance of my mom's look here, the way it's still '60s-influenced in her hair and eye makeup, while definitely of the '70s with that macrame belt. But my favorite part is knowing that I came along exactly nine months later. You can see it in Mom and Dad's gaze, can't you?"

The Couple: Carl and Debby Hagenmaier
Daughter: Wendy Hagenmaier
Era: 1977

"It was 1977 and my dad was Best Man," comments Wendy. "Donning the requisite baby blue tuxedo with polyester ruffles and brazen bow tie was a duty he accepted, without complaint. The mustache, however, is an accessory he added himself, by choice. When I looked at this photo with my Mom, she said, 'I love the man in the powder-blue suit as much right now as I did the instant Grandpa clicked the shot.' I may not emulate all of her styles, but I hope to emulate their love."

my mom,
THE PINUP

MYRNA STONE WILL NEVER FORGET THE OUTFIT SHE WORE one day in the summer of 1968. Neither will the entire U.S. Army: high-waisted short-shorts, a tank top dappled with daisies, and a headband. "I honestly have no memory of buying the outfit I'm wearing. I probably picked it up at one of the local department stores in Dayton, Ohio," says Myrna. "I usually covered up a little more than this, but my father-in-law, who was a professionally trained photographer, wanted to do a few "cheesecake" photos of me that he could send to Tom."

Tom, her husband, was stationed in Vietnam. "Tom actually received his draft notice about a month prior to our wedding and was supposed to report for induction two weeks before we wed," says Myrna. A little finagling allowed her college sweetheart to report for duty a few months later on Valentine's Day. "He was shipped out to Vietnam where he was stationed at Long Binh working 12-hour shifts in the underground United States Army Vietnam Communications Center."

His grueling tour of duty was made bearable by his correspondence with Myrna. "Before Tom left for Vietnam, he went to a local florist and arranged for one red rose to be delivered to me each month, along with a little poem that he composed and sent from Vietnam." So Myrna, in kind, sent him a photographic incentive to come home safely. But it didn't stay in his possession for long. "It kept getting stolen from his stuff, so she had to keep reprinting it and sending it again," says daughter Moira Stone.

But before long, everyone in the army had seen it. "That photo was chosen to appear by the editors of the *Stars & Stripes* as a regular feature—a 'here is part of what our guys are fighting to protect' kind of photo."

While Myrna was performing her civic duty in hot pants, she was also working two jobs saving up for her husband's return and launching her career as a published poet. "When Tom returned home, it was like we'd just gotten married all over again, only much, much better."

WEARING THE PANTS

It's not who wears them; it's who wears them better.

photo by Stephen Haynes

The Couple: Patricia and Stephen Haynes
Daughter: Emily Haynes
Era: 1970s

"My mom sewed her outfit—I love the sassy little gold belt. My dad seems to agree. The wall hanging behind them is now on the wall in my bedroom and constantly reminds me of all the adventures they had before they had me."

The Couple: Cullen and Kathleen Hewitt
Daughter: Kristen Hewitt
Era: Spring of 1972

"What I love about looking through old photos with my mom is the level of detail she can remember about her outfits, a lot of which she made herself. She made the lavender and white, geometric print, polyester knit outfit she's wearing here," says Kristen. "She had been very excited about purchasing the big navy blue purse, which came from a local leather goods purse maker, because the price was so good."

The Couple: Raffaella and Michael De Sola
Daughter: Claudine Gumbel
Era: Late 1950s

Raffaella's three-quarter length pedal pushers
were the original bike-messenger gear, with cuffs
short enough to avoid a chain entanglement. The
nineteen-year-old put her fashion sense into
practice in the Poconos, on her honeymoon in 1959.
Twenty-five-year-old husband Michael, a Wall Street
broker by day and a pompadoured rockabilly by
weekend, didn't mind the look one bit. Who wants
to bet the "let me teach you archery" bit was
his idea?

The Couple: Gwyn and Patrick Mannion
Daughter: Brenna Mannion
Era: 1981

The Couple: Francine and Tom Douaihy
Daughters: Christa and Margot Douaihy
Era: Early 1970s, Scranton, Pennsylvania

The inspiration for Francine's ruffled, cream-colored blouse was Paul Revere,
but not the horse-riding messenger. Rather, it was Paul Revere and the Raiders,
a garage rock band in the '60s that dressed up in Revolutionary War costumes.

"The outfit came from a clothing boutique where my cousin worked," says Francine.
"She was two years younger, gorgeous, tall and thin, with very short black hair.
She reminded me of Audrey Hepburn." Her cousin, a fan of the band, hand-selected
the outfit for Francine.

But the makeup was her own invention. "Yardley matte liquid makeup, vivid-colored
eye shadows like hunter green and royal blue plus white highlighter, and white
lipstick," she says. Overall, her style was London by way of Pennsylvania. As
for Tom, his look was simply Pennsylvania. And that suited Francine just fine.

The Couple: Ann and Toby Tobias
Daughter: Lacy Tobias
Era: 1970s, West Virginia

"I love that under the sheer shirt she's wearing a
striped tube top," says Lacy. "I see where I get my
penchant for interesting layering choices. I love
this picture so much that I had it framed for them
for Christmas a few years ago and it now hangs in
their hallway."

scrapbook:
THE PARTNERS IN FASHION

FOR THE GIANNI FAMILY, FASHION PAID THE BILLS. Eve Gianni Corio's parents' courtship began as a college romance and blossomed into a successful partnership as co-owners of a fashion label. Her mother, Diane, also served as the muse.

As a New York City kid, my mom Diane's interest in clothing developed at a rapid pace. She was weaned on shopping trips to Saks and nights out at the Copacabana. By the time I was in grade school, her style had eclipsed that of any other woman in New York City. My mom and dad actually met at the Fashion Institute of Technology—my father's mother was an off-the-boat Italian seamstress. In 1973, after marrying, the two decided to open a woman's clothing business, Gianni Sport, to provide the new woman's workforce with affordable and attractive business attire. This was around the same time as Donna Karan and Calvin Klein were getting into the business.

After their first big order from Macy's, they built a $50 million business and employed close to forty people in addition to installing about ten factories. My mom was listed in Crane's as having one of the most successful women-owned companies. When my father passed away in 1990, my sister dropped out of Parsons to help Mom run the company. I joined in 1995. It was our family business until 2004.

NOT YOUR FATHER

Old pictures of Mom are full of surprises. Where did that minidress go? When were you in Kenya? And who is that guy? In some cases, the answer is obvious.

Mom: Margaret W. Everhart
Daughter: Heidi Everhart
Mystery Man: Some guy who looks a lot like
   the actor James Garner
The Explanation: It's James Garner.

In 1957, Margaret won "The Most Beautiful Ears in the World" contest, and was flown out to Hollywood to meet with stars and do a photo shoot. At twenty-seven, her face was a dead ringer for Ingrid Bergman's, but it was her perfectly formed lobes that got all the attention. For the trip, Margaret stocked up on suits from Bonwit Teller, a high-end department store in New York. One was forest green with a collar made from real leopard. But nothing could compete with her ears.

Mom: Sylvia Ann Hewlett
Daughter: Lisa Weinert
Mystery Man: Bill Clinton.
Maybe you've heard of him.

The Explanation: "Cornel West and I had just published the book *The War Against Parents* in 1998," says Sylvia. "So we were invited to a White House dinner for a celebration. I wore a pink Luca Luca dress. And Bill and Hillary hosted the party."

7

Mommy and Me:
Growing Up with an Icon

In the relationship between mother and child there is a turning point. It's the moment, in your twenties or sometimes thirties, when you stop fearing becoming your mother and embrace it. But in the years leading up to that, it's a battle of wills. As a kid you may want to dress like your mom, and are mortally offended when she doesn't want to wear a matching teddy bear one-sie. As a preteen you may engage in epic tantrums over being banned from a low-cut tank top—or dating the girl in the low-cut tank top. As a teenager, you probably just learn to wear or do what you want on the sly. Point is, a lot happened between the time the kids in this chapter were born and the time they found these pictures of their moms, proclaiming them style icons.

LIFE IN THE SUBURBS

In a sea of matching houses and uniform lawns, sometimes the only marker
of individuality would come from Mom.

Mom: Indira Bolar
Son: Divya Bolar
Era: 1978, Shelton, Connecticut

"The sari is from Bangalore, India, the sunglasses are from Lord & Taylor's,"
says Divya. What separated her from the other suburban moms in the neighborhood
was 6 yards of unstitched silk that she'd wear to family functions and visits
with friends. "Back then there were not as many people wearing saris in America."
Indira had moved to the States in 1967 along with her husband, but she stayed
connected to her native country sartorially. "Much of her fashion inspiration
came from an Indian magazine called *Femina*," says Divya. Launched in 1959, the
magazine was a major fashion and culture resource for modern Indian women. For
Indira, it was a touchstone.

Mom: Bea Whitney
Daughter: April Whitney
Era: Early 1970s

"I was born when my mom was just twenty, and she maintained her youthful style while I was growing up. I love how she always looked so simply put-together—not a lot of adornment or fuss, just perfect. You'd never know that she was towing around a toddler and a diaper bag with her."

Mom: Laura Bobey
Son: John Bobey
Era: Late 1970s, Upstate New York

"Growing up, my mom had the reputation of a clotheshorse," says John. "But I think that's just because she cared about the way she looked in a family that was more 'utilitarian' in dress, shall we say? She was a single mom, so money was tight, and I know she spent money to make sure I was 'in style' more than she was." Style, of course, is subjective.

"My mom was always not just tolerant but encouraging of me expressing myself through the clothes I wore. I wore crazy hats, wild shirts, suspenders (a la Mork from Ork) and the like. There's a photo I love of her and me standing together at a birthday party. She's dressed in late-'70s Syracuse-meets-Studio 54, and I'm dressed as though I worked for the Ringling Brothers Circus."

Mom: Mary Ellen Conboy
Daughter: Deborah Giattina
Era: 1980

Mom: Erika Olson
Daughter: Elke Olson
Era: Mid 1970s

Clockwise from top left: In the 1970s before the kids were born. • In the mid 1980s with Reese's older sister, Laura. The entire Moore Clan in the early 1990s. • Christmas, 1981.

Mom: Patsy Moore
Daughter: Reese Moore
Era: The 1970s and 1980s, Florida

"While we always open our stockings in pajamas, it's an unspoken rule that the Moore family will be fabulously dressed after 10 A.M.," says Reese. "My mother used to give us hand-sewn, matching Christmas outfits, but later just settled for approving our adolescent selections."

Patsy, however, always won best-dressed. "She even looked great the year the plumbing backed up, the chimneys blew soot into the house, the heat went out, and we had six houseguests."

THE BABY ACCESSORY

Maybe it's the hormones, but mothers are best dressed in their postnatal period. After nine months of squeezing into trash bags, those cigarette pants are worn with a newfound pride. The little ball of human makes them look even better.

Mom: Jennifer Mitchem
Daughter: Paris Smith
Era: 1986, Orlando, Florida

"In the mid-'80s, my mom's days were dedicated to being my mom," says Paris. "She only worked nights as a hostess and never worked on the weekends so we could spend our days playing at the park or on the beach." Jennifer's style was a mixture of old and new. The shoulder-padded blouse was a staple of the *Working Girl* era. But the tartan cigarette pants were relics of the early 1960s. "Her creative style influenced me greatly, teaching me to never be satisfied by trends alone."

Mom: Mary Carter
Daughter: Lucy Carter
Era: Early 1970s, England

Usually it's the baby who's swaddled in a
blanket. But the wool poncho changed all that.

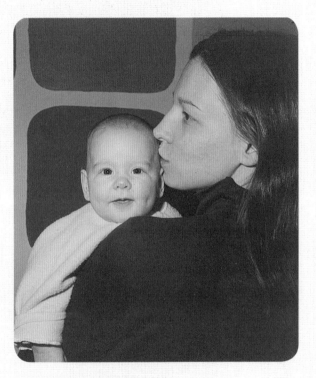

Mom: Patricia Haynes
Daughter: Emily Haynes
Era: Late 1970s

"I've always loved this photo of my mom—she is so
effortlessly beautiful," says Emily. "It was taken
just a few months after I was born, when my parents
were staying at a friend's house in Connecticut. My
dad had undergone surgery for Hodgkin's disease and
they were there to recuperate."

Mom: Marie Castleberry
Daughter: Sandy Lynn Davis
Era: 1970s

"From my first Christmas," says Sandy. "I'm pretty sure
my mom made the cute gingham dress she's wearing."

Mom: Ronda Crossett Provost
Daughter: Devon Geiger
Era: 1968, New York City

my mom,
THE MUSE

"WHEN I WAS SIX, I LOOKED LIKE A FIFTY-YEAR-OLD-WOMAN," Jess Rotter opines. Throughout her early childhood, she dressed exactly like her mother. Exactly. In Long Island in the '80s, mother-daughter fashions were hardly interchangeable. "She put me in a blazer and a brooch from Annie Sez for my fifth-grade yearbook picture." Then there were the matching tennis getups: "They were these nylon tennis suits called 'hot doggers,' that were pretty much $150 baggy 'Olympic' wear. My mom would call them the 'airplane outfits' because my entire family would wear these to the airport."

While she looks back on that period with more sympathy than admiration, it's just one chapter in a lifetime of taking fashion cues from her mother. Before Esther Rotter was "attacked by the '80s" as Jess puts it, she was a child of '70s Bohemia, heavily influenced by her Zionist fascination. "Her dream was to live in Israel, so in college she spent a semester on a kibbutz. I think she found herself there. She discovered the music of Cat Stevens and Chicago. Her life was so structured back home in New Jersey, but on the kibbutz she was surrounded by free spirits. Even the clothing was looser and unstructured. I think the aesthetic of Israel in the '70s was her biggest inspiration."

Like everything else, it had a trickle-down effect. A few years back, Jess created a line of T-shirts called Rotter and Friends, with drawings of musicians of her mother's generation, like Linda Ronstadt and Willie Nelson. Her illustrations capture the earthy psychedelia of the post-'60s era. "I always feel this comfort when I revisit the looks and sounds of that time," Jess says. "In the '70s everything was made differently, even the cheaper clothes were higher quality. People paid attention and put money toward visuals. Now everything is carbon copied. You can't tell culturally the difference from one city to the next."

As a child of the '80s, Jess did her share of mass-market shopping. "Retail therapy was the Rotter's answer to dealing with the tremors of life." By the mid '80s, Esther's husband was crippled by severe strokes. His illness took a toll on their tight-knit family, and Esther found ways to combat trying times with mother-daughter bonding shopping trips. "Once in a while, she'd take me out of school for a surprise trip to Loehmann's. It was one of my happiest moments from childhood. I'd find a top to wear the next day at school and that made everything okay for a time."

But a few years later, their fashion interests diverged. "I remember getting off the plane from college with a fake nose ring in, and she started screaming." Ten years later, Jess and Esther are returning to similar style ground. "She loves when I wear hippie clothing, as long as I look put together. The one thing she's always been adamant about is never to leave the house in sweatpants." Jess understands this as more than just a rule of thumb; it's a philosophy. "Going back to what she's gone through with my father, I understand the idea behind it: No matter what, put on a good front. She's a real survivor."

In the '60s as a teen in New Jersey.

The '80s attack: Jessica and Esther with matching sweater dresses.

Above and right: On her life-and style-altering journey through the Middle East in the '70s.

8

Moms Away!:
Sisterhood of the Traveling Pantsuits

Maybe when we return to the photos of our youth, it will seem like we took a lot of trips. But none more than our mothers. It didn't matter if they were flat broke or saddled with energetic toddlers; nothing stopped them from seeing the world. Unlike the contemporary accessories of adventure—backpack, camping stove, Tevas—these women packed an artillery of hats, dresses, and hip-hugging bell-bottoms. And they returned home with even more.

FREE BIRDS

No parents. No rules. The first taste of freedom never looked so good.

Mom: Audrey Both
Daughter: Amanda Both
Destination: Lebanon
Era: 1970

When Audrey arrived in Lebanon in 1970, she realized she may have packed too many minidresses. "The comments about my clothes were plentiful—the men liked what they saw; not so the women," says Audrey.

Her American style was a distraction to everyone she encountered, so after a few days, she bought jeans and some men's shirts to avoid the constant comments. Her elderly relatives were relieved.

Mom: Diane de Coppet
Daughter: Melanie de Coppet
Destination: France
Era: 1970s

"My mother and her sister Laura went to Brittany to visit
their sister, who was living abroad," says Melanie de Coppet.
"I have never seen my mother and aunt look cooler."

Mom: Marlene Weinstein
Daughter: Erica Frenkel
Destination: Key Biscayne, Florida
Era: 1971

This bikini was always a good luck charm for Marlene. "On a European trip
with my girlfriends, I met a guy while wearing that bathing suit. He was
gorgeous, and I couldn't believe he picked me," she says. "Later that year
the guy moved to Florida for pilot school, and I flew down for a vacation
with him. That relationship didn't last, but I loved that suit and wore it
till it literally shredded."

Southern California, early 1970s.

Honeymoon, St. Thomas, 1968.

Mexico City, 1972.

Mom: Kathleen Thacker
Daughter: Erin Thacker
Era: 1968–1972

Mom: Polly Kluttz
Daughter: Colleen Kluttz
Destination: The high seas
Era: 1966

As president of Alpha Delta Phi, Polly
captained a cruise for her sisters on
the Gray Line during their spring break
in Florida. Beyond bonding, it was an
opportunity for Polly to show off her
svelte figure in a new cocktail dress. It
was a departure from the outfit she was
best known for at her university: a giant
bird costume. "She was the mascot for the
football team, so she would dress up as
an ibis bird," says Colleen. "She always
complained that the head was very hot."

Mom: Janine Piniarski
Daughter: Dorothy Piniarski
Destination: Honeymoon, Canary Islands
Era: 1968

"My parents married over the holidays because my father was a sailor, and was shipping off for a couple of months," says Dorothy. "This was her first time flying anywhere, since she had grown up poor. Prior to this trip, her travels were by car, train, or boat."

"My folks both escaped Poland as teenagers, separately and from opposite sides of the country. They were eventually introduced many years later through a mutual friend in London."

Despite the photo evidence, Dorothy doesn't remember her mother dressing with the same panache. "I'm not sure why she stopped dressing stylishly. I blame motherhood and changing fashion trends clashing with her own style. She agrees, and also says that after I was born, she had a bunch of jobs that all had her wearing uniforms. Eventually, she became too tired to care about her appearance anymore.

"I always remember seeing this photo as a kid and noticing how she looked like a totally different person from the one I knew. It made me realize that she had a whole other life and sense of self before she started a family."

you were in trouble and did all she possible could to help in her own way.

Mom: Vivienne Davis
Granddaughter: Lindsey Davis
Destination: Acapulco, Mexico
Era: 1940s

"My grandparents were on their honeymoon in 1940," says Lindsey. "I love her sunglasses—they are the kind people spend hundreds of dollars on today. I also just love how happy she looks after all that she'd been through." Before she met Lindsey's granddad, Vivienne was engaged to another man who died of polio shortly before their wedding. "She said he looked like Errol Flynn. She always said she couldn't watch Errol Flynn movies because it was too much of a reminder." Her honeymoon was a turning point. Vivienne's mood elevated after months of mourning, and she was feeling hopeful again. Lindsay considers this picture one of her most precious possessions. It has accompanied her to every home she's lived in. Vivienne, now in her nineties, has her own relic from that period in her life: a pin engraved with the name of the first man she loved and lost.

The Airport

Mom: Ronda Crossett Provost
Daughter: Devon Geiger
Era: 1965

Whether you were a passenger or a stewardess, the only runway that mattered when it came to flying was the airport. For the plane ride to Iran, Ronda picked out an ornamental hat and a day dress with a fleur-de-lys collar. It was hardly an outfit you'd want to spend 15 hours sitting in on a cramped, bumpy journey over the ocean. But as a new recruit for the Peace Corps, it would be a while before she'd have the chance to get gussied up again. Besides, it was the freaking airport.

A Train Ride

Mom: Hilary West
Daughter: Emily West
Era: 1973, English countryside

"My mom was twenty-one and riding on the Vale of Rheidol steam train going from Aberystwyth to Devil's Bridge, a local beauty spot," says Emily.

Hitchhiking

Mom: Maureen Bailey-Green
Daughter: Natalie Bailey-Green
Era: 1967, Portsmouth, England

"She was just about to leave her home on the south coast of England to hitchhike to the south of France," says Natalie. "There she picked grapes and had fun with her best pal for six weeks."

A Cruise

Mom: Leonora Ivnitskaya
Daughter: Alla Ivnitskaya
Era: 1974, Moscow, Russia

"My mom loved travel," says Alla. "She left home
at seventeen to go to Chelyabinsk so that she could
get into the prestigious Institute of Culture in
St. Petersburg. She probably visited most cities in
the former USSR. Since borders were closed, people
couldn't really travel internationally." On this
particular cruise, Leonora, a college student at
the time, sailed to the southern port cities all
by herself, shopping in bazaars along the way.

photos by Curtis R. Schneider

Above left: At a dairy farm in California.
Above right: In Michigan in her favorite shirt.

A Cross-Country Road Trip

Mom: Patricia Victoria Larenas
Daughter: Carly Schneider-Clark
Era: 1978, California to Michigan and back again

In the late '70s, Carly's parents quit their jobs and spent a few months on the open road, picking fruit and working at farms along the way. "Her style reflected what I think was a 'back to the land movement' at that time," explains Carly. "Comfort and utility were important. She loved the straw-colored shirt, and she wore it constantly during the trip—it was warm and indestructible."

"The shot with the dairy cow is from when they were staying at a farm called Hidden Villa. I like this photo the best because it embodies the easy California style I have always tried so hard to emulate but can never get quite right. I used to look at all of these old photos and ask my mom why she didn't save her awesome bell-bottoms and knit sweaters for me. She looked at me like I was crazy. I don't think she thought of herself as very stylish—and that is what made her so."

my mom,
THE SUMMER ICON

ONCE UPON A TIME, LONG BEFORE HOLLY JORDAN WAS born, her mom Patti lived in a big house by the beach. With thirty other people. "It was a group house in Westhampton," says Patti Jordan. The kind that you had to be invited to join. "There was a whole interview process." In her early '30s, Holly's mom spent her weekdays working on Wall Street, and her weekends with her husband-to-be and a crew of other up-and-coming professionals who were anything but when they pulled off the Long Island Expressway.

"They threw the best parties. We'd always hire a band and at the time everyone drank rum," says Patti. "We had one 1776-themed party where everyone dressed in costume. One guy, dressed as Paul Revere, jumped over our fence on a horse." There was also the *Godfather*-themed party. "It was 1972 and the *Godfather* movie came out and made such an incredible splash." Patti bought a red sateen suit and paired it with her boyfriend's fedora. She even rented a 1920-style car for her arrival—straight out of another popular film, *Bonnie and Clyde*.

The red suit became a staple of Ms. Jordan's look through the years—making appearances on date night and Saturday afternoons. "It was a head turner." So was Patti.

The Georgia-born belle had moved to New York originally to work in the fashion industry. As a result, she developed a shopping habit that spilled over into costumes and sundresses for her summer respites.

"She has issues with my shopping. Every time I bring home a bag she goes, 'What did you buy now?'" says Holly, Patti's thirty-one-year-old daughter. "But looking at these old pictures of my mom, she clearly had her own addiction."

Patti does not deny this. "I loved to shop, but I always bought bright colors." That's a comment directed at Holly, if you didn't know. "It drives me nuts with her coloring," says Patti. "If you wear these beautiful shades of yellow and pink and turquoise, it brings out your hair and skin. I would encourage all young women to put some color around our faces." She also thinks Holly should get a summer share in the Hamptons.

TRAVELING WITH CHILDREN

Just because they were wrangling a stampede of hungry animals,
it didn't mean they had to dress that way.

photo by Yehudi Cohen

Mom: Rhoda Cohen
Daughter: Lisa Peet
Destination: If it's Tuesday, it must be Venice

By 1969, Lisa had moved to New Jersey. But a few years earlier, her life was a far cry from the eastern seaboard. "My dad, an anthropology professor, was teaching in Israel from 1966 to 1968, and we would take all sorts of side trips—to Italy, France, the Netherlands, and the United Kingdom. At that point, my mom was doing the faculty wife/mom thing."

She was also teaching her toddler about classic style—red car-coat, tights, and ballet flats made Lisa a dollhouse version of her mother. That didn't last for long. "While I admire it, her fashion sense did not rub off on me. If I had my way, I'd spend my life dressed like a twelve-year-old skateboarder." Blame Jersey.

Mom: Clara McGill
Daughter: Sarah Flizar,
the backseat photographer
Era: 1960s, suburban Chicago, Illinois

Clara turns a family road trip into
a Cary Grant movie, with the help of
accessories and nicotine.

Mom: Francine Douaihy
Daughters: Christa and Margot Douaihy
Destination: Nova Scotia, Canada, 1982

Being twins means never having to say you're sorry
for wearing the same outfit—as long as they're
different colors. Fraternal twins Margot and
Christa lived by this credo. Mom Francine had a
different rule: dress for the occasion. In this
case, that meant nautical-inspired. They had just
arrived in Nova Scotia by ship for their family
vacation. Aside from the red stripes on her shirt,
Francine was green the whole ride. "I was flat on
my back with severe seasickness, unable to leave
my bed until we arrived. We wound up driving
home thousands of miles up the coast, over New
Brunswick, and down the East Coast since I
wouldn't get back on the ship."

photo by Robert Mills

Mom: Mary Ann Mills
Daughter: Renee DeLuca
Destination: Hawaii on a family vacation, 1965

"My mom is a classic dresser—she taught me to buy good things
and take care of them and make them last," says Renee. "Better
to spend money on a good item and have it forever than to
replace something cheap over and over."

**Mom: Suzanne Kovacs
Daughter: Anne-Marie Kovacs
Destination: Central Africa**

In 1969, Suzanne moved with her family to the Congo. The Canadian native wasn't exactly thrilled with the prospect. "My dad is an engineer and was then in charge of the building of the Intercontinental Hotel of Kinshasa," says daughter Anne-Marie Kovacs. "Mom had not traveled much, and she had two little girls. The idea of moving to central Africa was overwhelming."

It also meant a departure from the creature comforts she was used to, like fashionable clothes. "I remember that we would come back to Montreal and take advantage of all the summer sales. We'd return to Africa with huge suitcases." Eventually, Suzanne got used to her new home, embracing it if not for the fashion, then for the parties. "Because there were no cultural activities, life was very social. In the end, I think that she might have had the time of her life while living there."

**Mom: Louise Swenson Mahoney
Daughter-in-Law: Tyrrell Mahoney
Destination: Athens, Greece**

Louise was already a world traveler by the time she became a wife and mother in the early '60s. This photograph from 1968 is typical of her fashion sense and style—so timeless and classic.

THE BELL-BOTTOM PERIOD. THAT'S HOW MY MOTHER, MARILYN, identifies the three weeks she spent traveling abroad with her parents. "In 1969, true bell-bottoms—the ones that broke off at the calf—were big. A year later, it was all about stove-top pants—which were similar but a bit more subtle. They flared out at the knee. But in 1969, on that trip bell-bottoms were what I wore," says Marilyn.

The vacation was far less planned than the outfits. The trip was supposed to be her honeymoon, but instead she'd called off the wedding. The gifts were returned; the reception reservation, canceled. The deposit lost. Her parents weren't too miffed—they never liked the guy. "My mother thought he had a weak chin," says Mom. So they invited her on a twenty-day European getaway to take her mind off things.

"Twenty days? Didn't you have a job?" I asked my mom.

"Yes I worked in advertising, but they were all sensitive to my situation." To say things were different back then is a gross understatement. One thing holds true: there's nothing like a good vacation to get your mojo back.

The twenty-three-year-old, now a free agent, embarked on a honeymoon with her folks. First stop: Israel. "The mood was spirited there, since it was only two years after the Six-Day War, and there was great sense of pride to be an Israeli." Tel Aviv, she describes as one big party—her nights spent in minidresses at local discotheques. On journeys to kibbutzes, she dressed in signature bell-bottoms for her 'gritty' one-with-the-soldiers experience. "I pretty much had a choice of any soldier I wanted." But all she wanted was fitted T-shirts—the kind that were unique to hippie kibbutzes in Israel. "I bought several of them to take home."

The next stop was Greece, where my mother posed before the Acropolis in an Indian headband and her signature bell-bottoms. "There was no question; I was an American. I didn't dress like anyone else there, but the response was very positive." A guy named Constantine took a particular shine. "I made the mistake of telling him to look me up if he was ever in the States, and two months later he was knocking on my apartment door. Turns out he looked better in Greece than in America. Those brown socks and pointy shoes didn't do it for me back home."

The final destination was London—the Emerald City of shopping in 1969. "The dollar was strong, so I went a little crazy." A brown floor-length wool coat with buckles, from BiBa, a high-end British label, went home with her. So did a Carnaby Street minidress. Throughout her travels, my grandma gawked at my mom's thigh-high hemlines and low-slung jeans. "I got a lot of attention from strangers, and my mom, who was a more formal, elegant dresser, was alarmed by the response." But she never dissuaded her daughter from wearing what she wanted. "Secretly, I think she liked the attention she got with me."

When Marilyn returned home, she was single, but she was also a woman who'd traveled the world—and looked like it. To thank her parents, she gave them a photo album of the trip. Dressed in fine jewelry and cashmere in the photos, my grandma looks like an elegant European heiress. My mother looks like a groupie traveling with the Rolling Stones. At first glance, they appear to be on completely different trips. They weren't, in the least.

At the Acropolis with her parents, Ruth and Irving.

At a London hotel on the last leg of her journey.

In Israel in a vest that came home with her.

Sporting her stovepipes.

Acknowledgments

This book would never have happened without the original, the brilliant, the beautiful Marilyn Weiss. Most mothers don't let their kids post pictures of them on the Internet without questions. Thank you for your tolerance, kindness, and above all—inspiration. I hope to be more like you every day.

My daddy, for not caring that he's pretty much not in this book. You are my best friend in the world.

My incredible sister Sasha, who taught me to write. I adore you. To Kassie and my baby Phoenix, who will totally worship his mom one day.

My very best friends, the other inspiration for this book. Never break the e-mail chain. Jessica, my creative life partner—let's get married. Colleen for making me funny—slacker girls 4 life. Margot, it's because of you I got this thing off the ground at all. Ryan, for making the proposal, the Web site, and the idea smarter. Meredith, for lending me your brain when I need it most. Lauren, for giving me espresso when I need it most. Don't underestimate it. Amy D., my rock and RockBand champ. Aimee R., whose style in both writing and dressing is always impeccable. Debbie, my cat's godmother. Michael, always a true friend.

My agent, Kate Lee, the genius. Is there a pill I can take that will make me more like you?

My editor, Emily Haynes, who turned one big panic attack into a cohesive book in seconds flat. You are welcome to do that for me every day. I'll pay you.

My cats, Wonton and BabyKat. I sure do wish you could read.

Ruth coming to accept her daughter's miniskirt and its consequences.

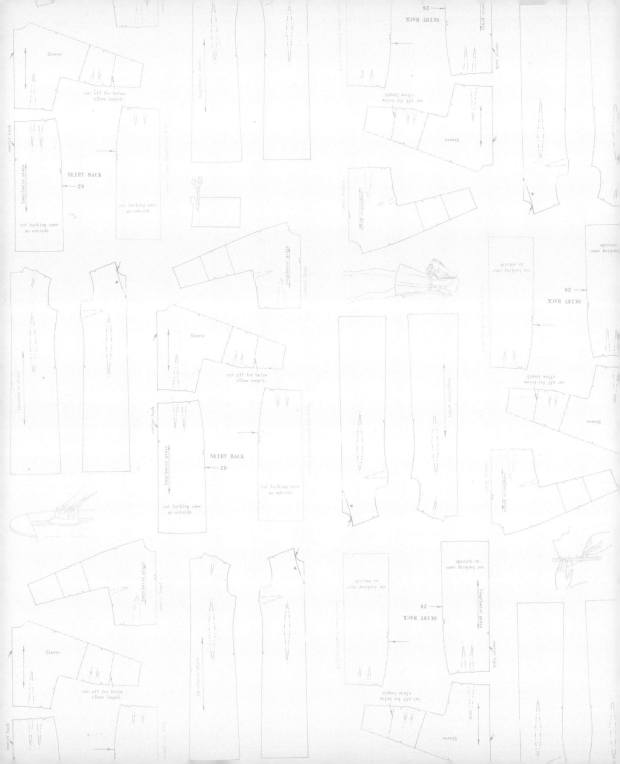